The Message Is Love

PENNY BLUE NORTH

NEWMAN SPRINGS PUBLISHING
320 Broad Street
Red Bank, NJ 07701

First originally published by Newman Springs Publishing 2022

ISBN 978-1-68498-793-1 (Paperback)
ISBN 978-1-68498-794-8 (Digital)

Printed in the United States of America

For Sunny. All things are possible.

CONTENTS

FOREWORD

Penny Blue North's *The Message Is Love* is a beautiful weaving of words from an enlightened point of view. Her writing is heartfelt and offers comfort like a hot chocolate on a cold night. Only from a place of pain can one find beauty in what someone perceives as difficulty. *The Message Is Love* is so important when unsure, confused, or when suffering, as it sincerely comes from a place of being raw and untempered to a place of wholeness. If you want to search for your own truth and find a way to surrender to what is, rather than what should be, then let this book be your guide. Surrender isn't throwing in the towel and saying, "I give up." Surrender is allowing *what is* to be evident to yourself without judgment. In doing so, Penny teaches the reader how to create their own best life and how to change the patterns they no longer want to see.

Moriah Rhame
How to Be a Happy Medium
Pendragon Publishing

INTRODUCTION

I'm not famous or brilliant. My training is in writing, not in psychology or philosophy. I am a regular middle-aged mom living in a small town, an evolving human mix of gifts and faults, studying existence through my own experience. At least that's what I did for the first half of my life. Now it's more like I am studying experience through my own existence. I wrote this book for my daughter as a guide for her spirit as she opens the door to college and the larger world beyond. As her most influential teacher, I would say she has earned an *A* in self-sufficiency, and she will function well in the world. She could run the place. As she leaves home, though, I find I have not finished teaching her how to know her soul. I've barely begun. I had to learn for myself, first, and it's been an amazing, if belated, journey.

When Eckhart Tolle *(Practicing the Power of Now, A New Earth: Awakening to Your Life's Purpose)* suggested that all fears manifest from our fear of death, I began to wonder. I had been harboring a terrible death-related secret for over a decade. When my father-in-law, whom I loved immensely, was waging a life-or-death struggle in the hospital, just before he died, we had two opportunities to file into the room and speak with him individually—once before a surgery that was to relieve encephalitis, the pressure and swelling of his brain, and once after that unsuccessful surgery. He was unconscious both times, but just in case he could hear me, I spoke fervently. The first time, I pleaded with him to hang on, to live for his granddaughter's sake. "She needs you. I need you. Please stay with us." I sang him a little song she had written about Cool Whip (she was just six years old) to remind him of the wonderful things going on in the world of the living, singing through a terrible headache that had come on when I entered the hospital that day. By my second private visit, though, it was clear that his physical body was beyond recovery, and I could not bear to imagine his pain. I worried that his suffering was being prolonged because he was trying so hard to stay alive for the rest of us, exactly the kind of thing he would do. If my own selfishness were contributing to this, I intended to stop it right then. So this time I said, with surprisingly great calm, "I'm sorry if you are in pain. It's okay if you need to go. We will be fine." It was as if someone else were speaking through me. He passed a couple of days later.

I didn't know where I found the peace I summoned that day. But at the time, and for twelve more years, I saw it as weakness. I hadn't known anything about death. Now I know that death teaches us about life. I didn't know it was possible to feel other people's emotions by mere proximity (and that I was really good at it, for better or worse). I didn't know that my father-in-law and I would continue to communicate after he passed. Now I believe that the dreams in which he appears are more than just dreams. Our private deathbed conversation was a source of guilt for a long time, and I never told anyone. What would the rest of my grieving family think if they knew that I not only approved of his passing but had quietly ushered it along? I believe now that I did him a great kindness, and that the calmness and grace passed both ways, initiated by him, to me, and back again. So perhaps it is more accurate to say that he did me a great kindness. He *was* in pain, he *did* need to go, and we *are* fine these many years later. I feel him close by, and he has been an even greater source of strength and comfort in death than he was in life.

I have never been one to take another's word for the truth nor to behave in a certain way because someone else says so. That's my own curse and gift. Life has had to hit me over the head (or literally break my back—see chapter 5) to teach me its lessons. I feel as though I have been dragged through hell, then dipped in heaven and set back down on the earth a new me. If nothing else of the old me exists, I remain an excellent student.

[A]lmost every belief I had embraced only hours before—that I was a physical being, that love was outside of me, that God was some patriarchal monarch sitting on a marble throne somewhere in the sky [trying to tell me what to do], that death was something to fear, that I was doomed by my past, that religion and spirituality were the same, that spirituality and science were different—was no longer true to my experience. Virtually every picture of reality I had used to define my existence—not to be confused with my life—had been cremated. The ashes of the woman I thought I was scattered to the wind.[1]

Lynnclaire Dennis wrote that. It's not only a damn good piece of writing, but it describes my sentiments exactly. I didn't have to survive a near-death experience to arrive at such a rebirth, as she did. You don't have to either.

I have been living this book. The lessons in it are simple and obvious. They also can be the most difficult things we do. Maybe there's something for your soul in this book too.

Tend the Negative

or

Your Teeth Are Beautiful; They're Just Crooked

or

Anti-In Charge

As you and your friend-siblings were growing up, Chaz liked to be left in charge if an emergency or quick errand called for me to be away. In time, his rank as oldest child held less and less clout because all of you were growing and maturing, each capable of being in charge, depending on the skills I was looking for. But Chaz liked to be left in charge. Once, he even demanded it. He was joking, of course—by then he was twenty-three and in law school—but it was a clever and touching joke, reminding me that I was still his mom 2.0, and he still wanted to be my sometimes-son. "If you don't leave me in charge, then I'm going to be *anti*-in charge," he laughed. "Instead of helping you, I will actively work against you." Chaz's joke illustrates what bullying is all about. Insecurities manifest as the need to control everything in the bully's environment, including other people. It is fear recast as manipulation.

The most obvious of bullies is the kind portrayed in school cafeteria scenes in movies. You know the ones. They seem to own the cafeteria and everyone in it, striking terror in the student body. Nobody is going to make a fool of them, until, of course, the hero of the movie does just that. The bully is unmasked to reveal the small, fearful boy or girl underneath. A less obvious but equally insidious bully is the regular, employed-with-a-family, obnoxious guy in the neighborhood. He, too, will not be made a fool of. He is always right, even when he is appallingly wrong. He consistently fires lawn services and paperboys for the slightest infractions. Nobody, besides himself, ever does anything right. Whereas the school cafeteria bully focuses on one or a few students to maintain control of the rest, the neighborhood bully cuts a wider swath. He is the cafeteria bully all grown up, still trying to control everyone and everything in his environment.

The most widespread bullying behavior, though, is not as easily recognizable and is practiced by the rest of us. Every time we are offended, insulted, or frustrated by the behavior of others, and we carry out, wish for, or design their punishment, we join the ranks of bullies everywhere. We hold grudges. We complain about injustice. We are great big babies who whine when we don't get our way. What a giant waste of time. I have wasted a lot of time.

It's raining outside, and as I walk past the windows, I see that my patio furniture, which is water-resistant but not waterproof, is out in the rain. I am instantly angry. I look for the source of my anger. Oh yes, the exterminator was here. He pulled the furniture out, away from the house, so he could spray insecticide at the base of the walls. How could he be so thoughtless? I don't go to his house and ruin his furniture. How could he do this to me? I used to spend my days in hundreds of moments like this. But really, did the exterminator set out to harm me? No. He pulled the furniture away from the wall to make his job easier and, very probably, to protect the chairs from the chemicals he was using. The furniture was already outside, so whether it was under the cover of the roof overhang, or twenty-four inches beyond it, was not something that crossed his

2

mind. Instead of looking for the source of my anger outside myself, I should have looked inside.

Whether I believe it or not, people do not set out to ruin my day. It is my own attitude that assigns intent, positive or negative. I can move the furniture back to the spot where I prefer it. I can talk to the exterminator and ask him to return it to that spot when he is finished spraying. I can ignore such a minor, meaningless outcome and enjoy my day. When I added up all the times that I held other people responsible for my bad feelings, I realized it was not injustice that made me angry. It was just stupid stuff, just things that didn't go my way. Though I never acted on these angry impulses, they had negative consequences anyway. They sometimes made me a nasty person. *I* sometimes made myself a nasty person.

My teeth were the perceived injustice that traumatized me well into my twenties. My baby teeth were nothing to smile about, and their removal, thanks to my mother's fear of them never falling out, produced a repeating cycle of wrestling matches (I swallowed a tooth in one of the terrifying struggles, feet defiantly wrapped around the legs of the coffee table under which I hid). But it was my permanent teeth that inspired the jeers of my siblings and tortured my self-confidence. Ever seen the ads for braces? The ones that show the most common issues requiring orthodontia? I had them all—overbite, underbite, crossed, sideways, a palate too small and teeth too big and numerous. Even with my mouth closed, a couple of teeth were so sharply sideways that they pushed my top lip out on both sides, hinting at a snarl.

And so, because I hated my teeth, I didn't take care of them. Brushing was minimal, and flossing, out of the question. It would have been like trying to moor in a coral reef. We had lessons in oral hygiene in health class at school. I chewed the little red tablet that showed all the food and plaque left on my teeth. I understood what I *should* have done, what the proper course of action was. But I didn't follow it because I just couldn't nurture something that was insistently hideous and ruining my life. Given a choice, I would have ripped the demons from my mouth and gleefully carried on with dentures. I was seven.

My teeth needed more care, not less. By the age of twelve, I had sixteen cavities. By twenty, my molars were literally falling apart. Living on my own by then, I saw a dentist, who said that what was left of two molars needed to be removed. He could replace them with dental bridges, or he could refer me to an orthodontist to fix my bite and straighten all my teeth. He favored the orthodontic route. "Your teeth are beautiful," he said. "They're just crooked." I wish I could remember that doctor's name because he changed my direction with a simple compliment. I had never for a moment thought of my teeth as beautiful.

I emerged after three years, full braces, a strategically broken palate, constant pain, and a week when my mouth was banded shut, with a lovely smile, not to mention a perfect bite, the disappearance of toothaches, meticulous oral hygiene habits, and elevated self-confidence. By tending the negative rather than shunning it, I recognized the positive that had been there all along. The pain was worth it. I should have mentioned that orthodontia becomes more painful as you approach adulthood, and your soft palate becomes "set." When you see middle-aged persons with braces, know they are enduring more pain than children generally do and more pain than I did. The monetary cost was worth it as well. Tending to the negative can require sacrifice and priority shifts. My pretty smile was not the end of the story, though.

Until I actually learned the lesson of tending the negative, my teeth were still calling the shots. I would look at other people who had crooked teeth and wonder what was wrong with them that they hadn't taken care of the problem. Worse, I judged them as somehow inferior based on a specious observation about something that was none of my business. Why did I have to suffer through orthodontia, but they could just walk around smiling and eating and being loved and living happy lives with their crooked teeth? What was wrong with everyone? This internal dialogue barely grazed my conscious thought, if at all.

If your mind ever presents you with "What's wrong with everyone?," chances are what's wrong is with you. In my case, I didn't understand that my teeth were not the actual problem. They were just doing what teeth do—biting and chewing as best they could from their slanted angles and responding to my lack of care. For this lesson, you could replace teeth with any body part, attitude, bad habit, or material possession. You have seen it in other people and maybe heard these things from your own internal dialogue: *I would be loved, if only…*

I had bigger boobs.
I were thinner.
I were smarter.
I didn't laugh so loudly.
I were on time.
I didn't sit around doodling all the time.
I had better friends.
I had a nicer car, wardrobe, house.

In other words, *if I were perfect*. Such is the language of perfectionism. A perfectionist is someone for whom perfection is the standard of value, and anything less is unacceptable. It follows logically, then, that for a perfectionist, *everything* is unacceptable because, really, nothing is perfect. Everything is negative, and nothing can be positive unless it is perfect.

Tending the negative means examining why it bothers you so much and what purpose it might serve. It doesn't mean excising everything that bothers you. Maybe that extra loud laugh is just what a film producer has been searching for, and it gets you a voice-over job, which leads to a career in film. Maybe a struggle with weight leads to an education in nutrition and a career in fitness. Maybe a doodler becomes a successful cartoonist. Maybe a little girl with crooked teeth grows up and writes a book in which those teeth become a useful metaphor in Chapter 1. I'm told that a mold of Freddie Mercury's teeth has been preserved in gold and that he credited his famous vocal range to his unusual mouthful of extra teeth. That weird thing about you, the thing that people make fun of, can become your signature, your blessing.

The constant conversation that goes on inside your head probably comprises some negative voices as well. Could it be that this internal negativity, too, serves some kind of purpose? I think so. For years, a voice I call critical mother has told me I was not good enough to risk speaking out, whether in the form of writing for my profession or communicating with loved ones. Oh how I hated that voice. It spoke with the sound of my real-life mother, though I know now that it's not really her but a caricature developed by my own subconscious. As I began writing my first novel in defiance of the voice, she doubled down on her criticism. Writing was torture. Every sentence had to be perfect before it hit the page. Now I know why so many great writers are also drinkers—the alcohol silences the internal critic. But I know what beast lives at the end of that road, so I didn't go there. I tried every other trick I could think of, though, to make her shut up. Nothing worked.

Finally, I just gave in, not to what the voice was saying (because I didn't believe it), but to the voice itself. If you want to talk that badly, I thought, then let's hear everything you've ever wanted to say. I allowed the voice to speak, and I wrote it all down. I put it right there in my book. She criticized my characters and their choices all day long. We got to know each other, which is to say I got to know a part of myself that constantly disagreed with the efforts of my conscious mind. Here was the bully, the anti-in charge person inside me. Could it be that she was simply doing her best, albeit from her slanted perspective? Could it be that she was actually beautiful, just crooked? Yes. Criticism was her way of protecting my vulnerability. If she kept me at perfection, I couldn't be hurt. Once I tended to the negative, it stopped being so negative. I let her know that I understood and appreciated the protection, but that I could handle it from here. It didn't happen all at once. It took about a year. Now I write and rhyme without fear.

An expert at tending the negative, Dr. Richard Schwartz, has developed the Internal Family Systems Model[SM], an approach to healing based on understanding the "people" inside us, our internal family, rather than attempting to bury or excise them. The model "involves helping people heal by listening inside themselves in a new way to different 'parts'—feelings or thoughts—and, in the process, unburdening themselves of extreme beliefs, emotions, sensations, and urges that constrain their lives. As they unburden, people have more access to *Self*, our most precious human resource..."[2]

I am still finding other distinct voices in my mind. Get to know yours. Don't believe what the negative voices say, but rather try to understand why they are saying it. They stand in a circle, forming a steely cage around your heart, using whatever they can to protect it. But a caged heart, though protected, can't do what a heart is made for—to love and to be loved. Tend the negative.

Practice Attention

"I'm cleaning up the dog shit before it snows tonight," was his greeting. I saw Shoopy in his yard almost every day on my morning walk, and the tending of our respective dogs or the weather was what our short, friendly exchanges had always consisted of.

"Yes, but I hear it's going to be seventy degrees tomorrow, after the snow," I said. Our relationship was about to change in marvelous ways.

"Where'd you get a piece of bullshit like that?"

"From the weather app on my phone." Rather than walking past, as usual, I stopped on the sidewalk in front of Shoopy's house. And I paid attention.

Shoopy has a lined face, a bald head, and a bulbous nose. He rather resembles Fred Mertz from the *I Love Lucy* show, if you can picture Fred Mertz swearing and picking up dog poop in the yard. And yet, when focused solely on him, I noticed in the contours of his face the expressions of people we hold dear. His nephew is your dad 2.0, his great niece your best friend-sister. I was close enough to his personal energy to feel his concern and love for his wife and dogs as he spoke of them. How is Evelyn going to recover from hip surgery? What will the dogs think of it all? Suddenly, he stopped.

"Do you hear that?" he said, raising a hand toward the trees. "That's a cardinal, that sound. I used to be able to whistle like a cardi-

nal, but now my false teeth move around, and I can't do it anymore."
I listened with him to the cardinal's song.

For a couple of minutes, I was present. I lived entirely in the
moment, focusing on nothing but Shoopy and the words he spoke.
Formerly, perhaps I would have been making a to-do list in my head,
half listening, perhaps bored, as he talked about things I assumed had
nothing to do with me. Polite, but not really there. It turns out we
are connected in ways I hadn't realized. I knew Shoopy was related
to our closest friends, but I had never before observed the strong
family resemblance and the same love of life his descendants share.
We love the same people after all. My own interest in birds is lim-
ited, coincidentally, to their sounds. And it seems that Shoopy and I
listen to sounds with the same intensity. This was my first conscious
experiment in practicing attention, and I was amazed. The only way
to describe the cause for amazement is that I felt, somehow, *fulfilled.*

Of course, we have no problems with living in the moment
when it's a big, positive, momentous occasion. The word *momentous* itself defines the feeling—of a moment. Think of the most
memorable positive moments of your life and the joy and sense of
being fully alive that accompanied them. How much of *you* imbues
those moments? None? All? Both are true. None, because at those
times your full attention is outside yourself, focused on other persons or activities. All, because the fulfillment—that sense of being
fully alive—is such a personal, selfish experience. It's amazing, isn't
it, how the outpouring of attention can be so fulfilling. The remaining billions of moments present similar opportunities for fulfillment.
When you think about it, *now* is the most expansive amount of time
we have, and the only time in which we can do anything. Wouldn't
life become wondrous if we could always live in the now? In that
kind of joy?

The same applies to the memorable negative moments of your
life. But in those times, your full attention is focused inward, on
yourself. You experience everything bad that happens as happening
to you. If it's bad enough, you feel even worse than the receiver. You
feel like the cause. In defense of your sanity, your mind may even

invite you to stand outside yourself, to view events as happening to someone else. It saves you from pain beyond what you can bear.

Most of us perceive time this way: When we experience time through the negative (the drudgery of work or school, sadness, grief, anger), individual days, hours, moments seem to last forever. Yet extended lengths of time pass us by (it's already New Year's and I haven't done anything with my life). Conversely, when we experience time through the positive (affirming challenges, quality activities with loved ones, happiness), individual days, hours, moments whiz by. It's why they say, "Time flies when you're having fun." You return to work on Monday, and though it's only been a weekend, it feels like you've been gone for months. You momentarily forget the names of people you just saw on Friday. Viktor Frankl writes about prisoners in concentration camps experiencing a "strange time-experience" where "a small time unit, a day, for example, filled with hourly tortures and fatigue, appeared endless. A larger time unit, perhaps a week, seemed to pass very quickly."[3] No matter who you are—victor or villain, no matter your location—penthouse or prison—you can determine how time moves.

When you practice attention, the simplest things become wondrous, and time stretches into an endless *now*. "[A]nything that we give our entire interest, attention and love to is the most interesting thing in the world, even if it's nothing but shaving and dressing."[4] Perhaps this is what Mother Teresa meant when she said, "Do small things with great love." If so, then attention equals love, and you can love life simply by giving it your attention. I have learned to make an art of activities I used to resent, like cleaning the barbeque grill and shaving my legs. I don't do them differently, but by giving them my full attention, they have become interesting, even enjoyable. This perspective is so new to me.

As the seventh of eight children, I had to fight for attention. Later, as a performer, I felt most comfortable when I could earn attention from an audience. Best if they ignored me completely until I turned their heads with a song. If people paid attention before I even sang a note, I would freeze with stage fright.

For most of my life, I viewed attention as something that was "paid" by one party (other people) and "earned" by the other (myself). I never sought unearned attention; in fact, unearned attention made me quite uncomfortable. I have been accused of backing away from attention so abruptly that I fell off a curb. On the other hand, I have also been accused of needing all the attention in the world. Both assessments came from people who were incapable of practicing attention (ah, the falseness of psychological projection), but nonetheless, their words made me think. Until recently, it never occurred to me to think in terms of reversed roles with myself as the payor and others as the earners because I always gave attention freely. People weren't required to earn it from me. At least that's what I thought. I wasn't as giving with attention as I have learned to be. And I had the whole concept wrong, anyway. Though it is valuable, attention is not something that has to be conserved, hoarded, withheld, competed for, or paid like a fee. It's free. It's better than free because its reward is hundredfold.

I'd been greeting some other neighbors, Burl and Martha, for about a decade, without having focused attention on them. Until the day I did. I had outbid Burl on an auction item the day before, a handmade wooden cross with intricate carved scenes of Jesus's walk to crucifixion. I have some friends who would love it, so I purchased it as a gift for them. When I saw Burl on the sidewalk, just returning home from his walk, I said, "Hey, I'm sorry I outbid you on that cross yesterday." He replied, "Oh that's okay. I already have one I'm going to hang in the living room—well, come here and I'll show you." He invited me into his home and said my dog could come in too. Inside, Burl produced another handmade wooden cross, explaining its expert craftsmanship as he showed me the different types of wood used to create it. He held it up to the wall to show where he intended to hang it, amidst the shrine of a son they had lost a couple of years earlier.

Now when I say that I had been greeting Burl and Martha for a decade, I must add that I knew nothing about them beyond which house they lived in and that they took a walk most mornings, because I hadn't given them any attention. In the next hour,

I learned all about their family, their grown children, and the son whose memory they cherished. After a while, Martha joined us in the living room, and we looked through photo albums of their son as we talked about the things he had loved. I was amazed at the depth of emotion they shared with me and at learning so many ways that we are connected. They happen to live next door to the friends I had bought the original cross for. Their son lived for music, especially the music performed at our annual community picnic. I was one of the performers of that music. I told Burl and Martha I hoped I had done justice to his memory. I've since been told that inviting neighbors in off the street is not something this couple has ever been known to do. I felt so honored to be invited into their lives and hearts. We never know when we are going to touch someone deeply, or they us.

I had been practicing attention for a few weeks by the time Burl invited me in to see the cross. Whereas before I would look at people, make a quick (but subconscious) judgment, and then forget them, I had begun really looking at people, seeing past their physical traits and wondering what they might be going through. You would be surprised what a change you can make simply by picturing every other person as yourself. For me, it began as a metaphor for the idea that everyone is on a journey and acting not necessarily as they want to but as they believe they must. "There goes me," I would say. "And there's me too." "There's me. I'm old. I can't walk very well." "There's me, and I'm keeping my head down so people won't notice me." I began to feel like I was psychic, like I could almost grasp what people were dealing with. But it's really just a matter of close attention. If the reincarnation of souls is real, then seeing everyone else as myself becomes more literal. Maybe I have lived or will live in that body, and maybe I will learn something from experiencing life from that perspective. Even if we don't reincarnate, practicing attention here and now in this body is a learning experience. I am *in* the world, not apart from it.

I am convinced that practicing attention creates a shift in our energy vibration and can affect those around us. People are drawn to positive energy. My proof of this is that a lot of strangers now come up and speak to me in public. That didn't happen before I started practicing attention. Positive energy is like sunlight. All living things are drawn to it. Plants and animals don't have a choice about it; they don't consider whether growing toward the light is a good idea. They just do it. Human beings, on the other hand, though naturally drawn to the light, can willfully turn away from this life-giving energy. Don't.

Practicing attention can heal. In the middle of receiving a massage, I was focused on the moment. I thought of nothing beyond the expert treatment my therapist was rendering and how great it felt. If you really want to live, live in the now, in this very moment. All your experiences will be magnified, as this massage was for me. As Kim worked on my sacral area, her hands felt hot, as if she had taken stones from a fire and was moving them across my back. Maybe she was doing some kind of stone treatment. If not, I wondered what could produce this kind of heat, and I could have asked Kim right then, but I wanted to remain in the moment. After the massage, I said, "At no time were you using hot stones on me, were you?" Kim immediately became contrite. "Oh, I'm so sorry," she said. "Was I supposed to be doing a hot stone treatment? I'm sorry. It's just that my father is dying, and I just felt so depleted this morning." I assured her that I had not requested hot stones, that she did everything just right, and that I was trying to figure out where this tremendous heat came from, and did it originate with her or me. Kim had felt the heat too, and she recognized it as energy emanating from me. "You must need it," I said. "Come and take it all." We hugged for a long couple of minutes while she cried out her pain. How wonderful that I could give her the energy she needed to replenish her strength in dealing with her father's passing. And I marvel that giving such energy did not take anything away from me. On the contrary, I felt energized. Yet I don't have any special powers. The energy was not being created by me so much as moving through me. It's all because I practiced attention.

Speak Up

I didn't think I could be hypnotized, controlling as I tended to be. The doctor told me not to worry about it, that it wasn't a test, and I could not fail at it. She said that whether I actually believed I had lived the lives we would explore, or thought they were merely figments leaked from my subconscious, it didn't matter. Whatever came out would be what I needed to know, and the associated emotions were most important.

Doctor: Picture a door in the garden. What does it look like?

Penny: Just a plain brown door.

Doctor: A plain brown door? Anything else? Does it have a handle or knob?

Penny: A knob on the right side, so that you have to open it with your left hand.

Doctor: Okay, open the door and step through to a time in your childhood… What do you see?

Penny: I'm playing in the dirt.

Doctor: How old are you?

Penny: I'm three.

Doctor: Is anyone with you?

Penny: No… My brothers and sisters are somewhere else.

Doctor: They're somewhere else?

Penny: Yes. I'm barefoot, so I couldn't run off with them. (*This is a conscious memory. I'm not hypnotized. I remember perfectly.*)

Doctor: Is this a place you know?

Penny: It's on the farm. I'm too little to go with them.

Doctor: Are you upset about that?

Penny: No. I like playing in the dirt. I make up people.

Doctor: What kind of people?

Penny: All kinds. I make them up and play stories with them.

Doctor: What are you wearing?

Penny: I don't know.

Doctor: Are you close to any of your siblings?

Penny: Margot takes care of me.

Doctor: She takes care of you?

Penny: Yes. She bathes me and feeds me.

Doctor: Is she there now?

Penny: Yes.

Doctor: What is she doing?

Penny: She just gave me a bath, and she is putting powder on me. I got a shot, and she is trying to tell me I don't know which butt cheek I got the shot in. She is trying to make me forget.

Doctor: Why did you get a shot? Are you sick?

Penny: No. Just a shot at the doctor. She is trying to make me forget about it. But it still hurts. I know which side it's on.

Doctor: What is she doing now?

Penny: She is helping me get dressed. I have blue corduroy pants with a pocket in the front. I'm afraid the other kids will make fun of me because usually the pocket goes in the back. (*But I'm three*). I don't know what kids because I'm not old enough to go to kindergarten.

Doctor: That's okay.

Penny: I also have an orange shirt dress. It's new. It looks like a shirt, but it's a dress. (*I want to tell her more about the new clothes I got because they are my first new clothes that I remember*).

Doctor: Are your parents there?

Penny: My mom is in the house.

Doctor: What is she doing there?

14

Penny: She's making pies.

Doctor: Making pies? Is this something she does often?

Penny: No.

Doctor: Is this a special occasion then?

Penny: It must be Thanksgiving or something.

Doctor: Is this a pleasant memory for you?

Penny: Yes. She gives me little pieces of dough to put sugar and cinnamon on and bake.

Doctor: Is your dad in the house?

Penny: No. He's outside on the tractor. (*Now I am outside again*). It's summer now. (*How can it be summer outside when it's Thanksgiving inside?*)

Doctor: That's okay. That's fine. Is he on the tractor a lot?

Penny: Yes. He works the land.

Doctor: Working the land, is that something he enjoys? (*I can smell the tractor grease. Tears start flowing from my eyes, and I don't know why*).

Penny: Yes. I don't know why I'm crying. This is a good memory.

Doctor: That's perfectly fine. Let's go back to the garden now. Picture another door. Can you tell me what it looks like?

Penny: It's a metal door, a gray metal door with rivets all around it.

Doctor: Okay, now step through this door and tell me what you see.

Penny: I see white marble and pillars and a crescent-shaped pool.

Doctor: A pool for swimming?

Penny: No, a decorative pool. It's not deep.

Doctor: Where are you?

Penny: I don't know.

Doctor: Are you inside or outside?

Penny: Well, both. It's open air, but it's a building (*I want to say palace but I don't*).

Doctor: Is it your home?

Penny: Yes.

Doctor: How old are you?

Penny: I'm five. (*Where did that come from?*)

Doctor: What are you wearing?

Penny: I don't know.

Doctor: Is there anyone with you?

Penny: No. (*Then in my peripheral vision, I see a man walk by*). Yes.

Doctor: Who is it?

Penny: I don't know him.

Doctor: What does he look like?

Penny: A soldier.

Doctor: Why is he there?

Penny: I don't know. Probably to see my father. (*Why?*)

Doctor: Does your father have something to do with the soldiers?

Penny: Yes.

Doctor: In what capacity?

Penny: He's in charge of them.

Doctor: Is he a general?

Penny: No. He's not a soldier. He's in charge of everybody. He is the leader. There's a dog, a white dog. She's an Afghan.

Doctor: An Afghan?

Penny: Yes. It's the kind of dog with long hair and a long nose.

Doctor: Is it your dog?

Penny: Yes. But it's not a dog for playing with. It's to show to others.

Doctor: Who told you that?

Penny: My father. (*Again, where did that come from?*) We're going to get muddy. And we're going to get in trouble.

Doctor: You're going to get muddy? How?

Penny: We're going to go play in the field, and we're going to get muddy, and we're going to get in trouble because we're not supposed to get muddy.

Doctor: Who are you going to be in trouble with?

Penny: My father. I feel like I'm making this up.

Doctor: That's perfectly okay. Is your father going to treat you badly?

Penny: No. He's going to say I'm not supposed to play with the dog and get muddy. (*Then I'm standing before my parents with the dog, and I'm all muddy*).

Doctor: Is your mother there?

Penny: Yes. She's beautiful.

Doctor: How does she feel about you getting muddy?

16

Penny: She thinks it's funny, but she can't show that in front of my father. I know what I'm wearing now. It's like a sack. Or a pillowcase.

Doctor: Okay. What happens after you get in trouble for being muddy?

Penny: The girls come in and take us away. They have dark hair. One of them is Margot.

Doctor: What do the girls do?

Penny: They bathe me. They get the dog clean.

Doctor: Are they family members?

Penny: No. They work there.

Doctor: They work there?

Penny: Yes. They work for my father. They take care of me.

Doctor: Okay, let's go forward in this life to the next important event. Where are you?

Penny: I'm outside. There's a lot of wood now. Walls.

Doctor: How old are you?

Penny: I'm a teenager.

Doctor: What are you wearing?

Penny: I don't know.

Doctor: Look at your feet. What kind of shoes are you wearing?

Penny: I don't know.

Doctor: What do you see?

Penny: A cannon of some kind. It's big.

Doctor: Why is it there?

Penny: It's for the battle.

Doctor: Is there going to be a battle?

Penny: Yes.

Doctor: Is someone invading?

Penny: Yes.

Doctor: Who is invading?

Penny: I don't know.

Doctor: Are they invading a country? An island? A village?

Penny: (*Don't say it—it sounds stupid*) No. A kingdom.

Doctor: Your kingdom?

Penny: My father's kingdom. He's the king.

Doctor: So you're preparing for a battle?

Penny: The soldiers are.

Doctor: And your father is in charge of the soldiers?

Penny: No. He's too old now. There is a younger man in charge now.

Doctor: Who is it?

Penny: His name is Swen. He has dark hair. He's very handsome. (*I know who he is in this life, but I don't tell her because it sounds made up*). He is in charge now.

Doctor: What are you doing with the cannon?

Penny: Nothing. I'm just looking at it. It's going to kill a lot of people.

Doctor: Are you married?

Penny: No.

Doctor: Is there someone you are interested in?

Penny: (*Swen's face comes to mind, but I don't say it*) No.

Doctor: What do you like to do?

Penny: I like to write.

Doctor: You like to write. Like historical writing?

Penny: No. Stories. I like to write stories.

Doctor: Oh, Okay.

Penny: And I'm grateful to be able to do it. People don't have paper. I have all the paper I want because (*I want to say we're royalty, but I don't*) we have access to it. Other people don't. I can see my sandals now. They're silver and they shine.

Doctor: What is significant about your sandals?

Penny: Nothing. I just like them. (*I want to say that I'm the only one who has sandals this nice, but I don't*).

Doctor: What do you like about them?

Penny: I bring my knees up and wrap my arms around my legs and look at them. They're pretty. I like to look at my sandals and write my stories.

Doctor: Okay, let's go forward in this life to the next significant event. What is it?

Penny: My mother is dead. It's her funeral. (*I start crying*).

Doctor: Is your father already gone?

Penny: No. He's still alive. He's very old.

Doctor: What are you doing?

Penny: Walking up to her body (*I can't stop crying*).

Doctor: Is anyone with you?

Penny: Ivan.

Doctor: Who is Ivan?

Penny: He's my husband. He is trying to comfort me, but he doesn't give me what I need. I feel so alone (*I am now absolutely bawling*).

Doctor: Let's back up a little bit in this life, to a time when you are first married. Is your husband there?

Penny: Yes.

Doctor: Who are you married to?

Penny: Ivan. He's Justin.

Doctor: Who's Justin?

Penny: My nephew, Justin. It's him. He likes to drink (*I can see him in the great hall, drinking with all the other guys*). He likes to have fun. I don't love him, though, not romantically.

Doctor: You don't love him?

Penny: No. I like him. He is a good man. I don't love him.

Doctor: Do you have any children?

Penny: No.

Doctor: Does he treat you badly? Is he not affectionate?

Penny: No, he treats me fine. He is affectionate. I just don't love him. He doesn't take care of himself. He likes to drink.

Doctor: And that bothers you?

Penny: No, it doesn't bother me. It's okay. I go to bed early because I want to look good in my blue dress. He stays up with the other soldiers.

Doctor: Is the blue dress for a special occasion?

Penny: I don't know.

Doctor: Ivan is a soldier?

Penny: Yes. He is very important, and he has a lot of men he is in charge of. But he is not the leader. He is like a general or something.

Doctor: Is there someone else you would rather be married to?

Penny: Swen.

Doctor: Why aren't you married to Swen?

Penny: Because I never said anything.

Doctor. You didn't make your feelings known?

Penny: No.

Doctor: Why not?

Penny: I don't know… I don't think Swen notices me…

Doctor: Okay, let's go forward to the last few minutes of this life. Where are you?

Penny: I'm in bed.

Doctor: Is anyone with you?

Penny: Yes, my dog. She's a black-and-white spaniel. Her name is Hester.

Doctor: Are you sick?

Penny: I'm very old. My whole left side hurts. That's why Hester is lying there. She knows. She is a good dog.

Doctor: Is there anyone else there?

Penny: The girls. The ones who took care of me when I was little. They're old themselves now. But they're still there.

Doctor: Is this the home where you grew up?

Penny: I don't know.

Doctor: Is Ivan there?

Penny: No. Ivan died a long time ago.

Doctor: How did he die?

Penny: In the war.

Doctor: Okay, what happens when you die in this lifetime?

Penny: I float up above everyone. (*I feel elated! I want nothing, nothing at all, but to remain in this state, but she keeps asking questions*).

Doctor: What happens after you float up?

Penny: Hester is sad because I died, but she will be okay. She will go with the girls. She's such a good dog. She is sad, but she's okay.

Doctor: What would you say are the lessons you learned from this life?

Penny: To use power wisely and to speak up.

Doctor: What do you mean by "use power wisely?" Did you not use power wisely in this life?

Penny: I did for others. I gave a lot of money to poor people. I helped a lot of people. But I didn't help myself. I didn't speak up. (*All*

20

*I would have had to do was tell my father I wanted to marry Swen
and I could have. I could have had anything I wanted*).

Doctor: Let's go back to the garden now and visualize another door.

Penny: It's not a door. It's a doorway, with a white curtain blowing
in the breeze.

Doctor: Okay, walk through the doorway and tell me what you see.

Penny: Nothing. It's green. Green grass.

Doctor: Where are you?

Penny: It's just a green field, like *Little House on the Prairie.*

Doctor: What are you doing there?

Penny: I'm looking for something. (*How did I know that?*)

Doctor: What are you looking for? (*Suddenly, I see what I'm looking
for, as she comes running up to me, an adorable little short-haired
dog.*)

Penny: My dog. Her name is Pippi or Peppy or something like that.

Doctor: (*She asks me another question, but I am busy trying to think of
the dog's name.*)

Penny: It's Pepper. My dog's name is Pepper, which is funny, because
she's white. It's because when she was a puppy she got into the
pepper, so we named her after that. She has an injury to her left
hind leg, so she limps. She is a troublemaker.

Doctor: How old are you?

Penny: I don't know. Eight or nine.

Doctor: What are you wearing?

Penny: I don't know.

Doctor: Do you see your house where you live?

Penny: Yes. It's made of wood. Like a cabin.

Doctor: Who lives in the house with you?

Penny: My mother. It's the same mother from before. She looks the
same.

Doctor: Is there anyone else there?

Penny: My sister, Elsa. I think I have two sisters, Elsa and Elizabeth.
(*I try to think of my own name, but it doesn't come to me.*)

Doctor: What are you doing there?

Penny: We're cooking.

Doctor: Is your father there in the house?

Penny: No, he's out hunting with my brothers.

Doctor: What does your father look like? Is he tall? Short?

Penny: (*I laugh.*) He's short. He looks like Snuffy Smith from the comics. But my brothers are big, much bigger than he is. They are hunting. Rabbits, I think. Pepper isn't allowed to hunt with them. She's too much trouble.

Doctor: Plus she's injured.

Penny: Yes.

Doctor: Let's move forward in this life, to a time when you might be married. Where are you?

Penny: In my house.

Doctor: The house you grew up in?

Penny: No, my own house.

Doctor: What are you doing?

Penny: I have to make all these pies and all this food.

Doctor: You're making pies?

Penny: Yes. I have a lot of work to do. (*I can see my daughter there, but I don't mention her.*)

Doctor: Why do you have to do this?

Penny: It's for the church. I have to do all the work because my husband isn't here. I would rather be playing my piano.

Doctor: Where is your husband?

Penny: He's on a fishing trip. He's on a boat with my brothers. They work together.

Doctor: He's on a fishing trip?

Penny: Yes…but he's not coming back.

Doctor: He's not coming back?

Penny: No. He left me. My brothers will tell me that there was some kind of accident and he drowned, but it's just to spare my feelings. I know he left. I told my brothers to bring the piano downstairs because the heat upstairs isn't good for it. I would rather be playing the piano. He's gone, but I don't care.

Doctor: Why do you think he left?

Penny: I don't know. I don't care. He was a sharp dresser. He fooled a lot of people, but he didn't fool me.

Doctor: He fooled a lot of people?

Penny: Yes.

Doctor: Let's go forward in this life. Where are you?

Penny: I'm floating up above the church. There's a big picnic going on.

Doctor: Is that why you had to make all the food?

Penny: No. This is a different picnic. My daughter is married now. She is with Kenneth. I can see them.

Doctor. You have a daughter?

Penny: Yes.

Doctor: Who is Kenneth?

Penny: Her husband. She is okay. She is happy.

Doctor: Is this after you die?

Penny: I don't know.

Doctor: Why do you think you are floating above the church?

Penny: I don't know. I'm very churchy. I do a lot for the church. I play the organ, and I sing in the choir, and I organize a lot of charities. And I make a lot of food for events. Everything seems to be going well at the picnic, so I'm satisfied about that.

Doctor: Okay, let's go back to when you are making the pies. Is your daughter there?

Penny: Yes. Her name is Maisy or Maybell or Mabel. Something like that. She has a limp.

Doctor: Did something happen to her?

Penny: No. She was born that way. She limps, but she's okay.

Doctor: What is she doing?

Penny: She is making paper dolls for her father for when he comes home. She's out on the porch in the rocking chair. But he's not coming back. She doesn't know it.

Doctor: (*She asks another question, but I feel like I have to confess about my daughter.*)

Penny: I love her, but I bet she thinks I don't.

Doctor: Why would she think that?

Penny: Because I don't have time to spend with her. I love her, but I don't spend time with her because I have all this work to do because my husband is not here. (*Oh my god, to her, I am like my mother was to me in this life.*)

23

Doctor: (*She starts to ask another question, but this word pops out.*)

Penny: Arthropods.

Doctor: Why did you say that? (*You're asking me? I don't even know what it means!*)

Penny: Arthropods. That's what my daughter is interested in. But I don't pay attention to her.

Doctor: They're insects. Bugs.

Penny: Well, that's what she likes. I do love her. I just don't have time.

Doctor: Let's move ahead in this life to the few minutes before death. Where are you?

Penny: I don't know.

Doctor: What do you see?

Penny: Nothing…a bucket of water.

Doctor: What is it for?

Penny: I don't know. It's just there.

Doctor: Are you in bed?

Penny: I think so.

Doctor: Are you in your house?

Penny: I don't know. My nose (*on the inside*) feels like it's burning. My nose and my throat are on fire.

Doctor: Did you drink something? Did you take something that would hurt you?

Penny: No. The bucket of water is so they can dip cloths in it and put them on my body. I feel like I'm burning up.

Doctor: Are you sick?

Penny: I'm feel like I'm burning. I can't sing. My throat. I don't want to live if I can't sing. (*I start bawling again. I really feel like I don't want to live.*)

Doctor: It's okay. Can you speak?

Penny: I don't know… I think I can, but I choose not to.

Doctor: (*Tries to guide me to the moment of death, but I don't actually get there—maybe I was there before, floating above the church.*) What would you say are the lessons you learned from this life?

Penny: That I can't have it both ways. I can't say I don't care about my husband leaving, yet blame his leaving for my problems. I have to speak up.

Doctor: Okay, what else?
Penny: To take care of my daughter, pay attention to her.

The doctor was right—about the emotions, I mean. When I left her office, I turned up the radio in my car as loud as it could go, and I sang all the way home. I had just suffered two lifetimes of failure to speak up, not to mention waking up to self-inflicted silence in this one. It will never happen again. Now you know what inspired me to make a vow to you and the rest of our family—"Never again."

The doctor was also right about the source of the stories. Whether these are lives I actually lived or the stuff of my subconscious, much of it was focused on speaking up, which I realized I had failed to do for so long.

I can't guarantee that you will get what you want if you speak up about it. The whole point of this book is to accept and learn from that which you cannot change. But if you speak up, you will live without regret, without expending futile mental energy trying to calculate what *might* have happened. Say no to what you don't want. The great benefit is self-respect, which beats fear of not being liked every time. Speak up about small things. If you don't like pepperoni on your pizza, say so. Your friends won't abandon you over it. If you do like a silly television show, enjoy it, don't hide it. And speak up about big things—to loved ones who have hurt you, about whom you love, for what you think is right.

Seek Balance

Until now, I've never been one to do things in moderation. I lived in extremes. I would read a book in one sitting, even if it took all day and night. I would work out every single day, with no days for rest. I was fine with eating no potato chips or eating all the potato chips, but not just a few. In group projects, especially ones that were graded, I would take on the work of the whole team in order to earn the *A*. I loved and hated fiercely. I was for one or the other, of anything, but never both.

Once, in order to prove I could do anything in moderation, if necessary, I placed a bowl of hazelnut chocolates on my desk at work and ate one a day until they were gone. (Only now do I appreciate the irony of thinking that "proving" something would have anything to do with moderation.) "There," I proclaimed, after thirty days. "That was the most boring month of my life." I needed to be right, to show that I could change if I wanted to, and that moderation was for everyone else but not for me. The truth, though, was that I could not have changed back then. What propelled me to success with the chocolates was that it was a challenge from my office mate and friend—and I always had to win. As any of my former employers could tell you, the most effective motivation for me was a direct challenge, and the reward needed be nothing more than bragging rights. Here are some insights offered from a few of those employers:

"If you can't win, you don't want to play."

"You are the queen of the grand statement."

"If it's not perfect, you throw it in the trash."

"You have the most alcoholic personality I've ever seen in a person who is not an alcoholic."

Competitive was the positive name I gave to my dependence on comparison with others. Because competition is a good thing. It's good in business, economics, and sporting events. It makes games and recreation more fun. It can bring out the best performance in the competitors. But you have probably noticed it can also bring out the worst in people. When that happens, it is due to a lack of balance.

Finding balance at the behavioral level can be nearly impossible, though, because day-to-day, automatic behavior is wrapped in layers around core beliefs you might not even be aware of. My problem was not the fact that I couldn't eat just a few potato chips at a time but the beliefs I held deep down, which spread outward in all directions and resulted in that kind of extreme behavior. If you are having trouble balancing work, school, and family, chances are the problem isn't work, school, or family but something inside of you.

Look at where you stand on the virtues and vices. I'll use the seven deadly sins and their corresponding virtues as a place to start.

Pride

Pride is the state of being proud. One definition is inordinate self-esteem or conceit; another is justifiable self-respect. One is delight or satisfaction derived from some action, possession, or relationship; another is disdain. Pride is the recognition that you are of value and that of any achievements open to you, the one that makes all others possible is the creation of your own character.[5] Or, pride is an inflated sense of your own worth or personal status and typically makes you feel a sense of superiority over others and can easily make you look condescendingly at others.[6] Depending on who you ask, pride is a sin or a virtue.

Pride's opposite is humility, the state of being humble—a spirit of deference, lowliness. Humility is a deflated or defeated sense of self-esteem, a feeling of inadequacy. Or, humility is the proper stance of a human being toward life on earth, a recognition that we are small in relation to the awe of nature and God. Again, both answers are out there. At your school, I noticed a sign outside a classroom that says, "You Are Special." At the same time, one of your teachers is famous for this rejoinder: "You think you're special? Well, you're not." The messages are mixed to achieve balance. Some kids need to be pulled toward the center from defeat, so they are reminded that they are more special than they believe. Some kids need to be pulled toward the center from conceit, so they are reminded that they are not as special as they think they are.

Find virtue and vice in both qualities. Don't be conceited, and don't be defeated. You are not below all others, nor are you above all others. I'm not saying that you should walk the center line, always exactly halfway between pride and humility, but be proud and humble, respectively, when you deserve them. Don't base your worth on a comparison to others. You are already enough. Your self-esteem is not a competition.

Greed

Greed is an intense desire for more than is needed, especially money, power, or food. It is rapaciousness, covetousness. Or, greed is a desire for more than is rightfully earned. It depends on where you place *need*. At an extreme, all we need is minimal food, shelter, and clothing, so a desire for anything beyond the caveman lifestyle constitutes greed. On the other hand, what we earn by our own hands, hearts, and minds is what we deserve, and greed extends only to that which we don't deserve—the possessions, power, and relationships of others. Greed comes from an imbalance on the self-esteem scale and produces that other deadly sin, the emotion of envy.

Greed's opposite is altruism, charitable acts that promote the welfare of others at no benefit, and even at harm, to the giver. At the extreme, altruism is considered virtuous *only* if giving does not benefit the giver. From this perspective, charitable donations don't count if you can afford them, and giving for the sheer pleasure of it doesn't count either.

Balance your giving. What you earn is yours, and what you give is at your pleasure. If you lack balance on the self-esteem scale, you may be known as greedy, no matter how much you give, or you may feel put upon because your sacrifices are not recognized. If you are comfortable on the self-esteem scale, you may be known as a generous person while simultaneously feeling like you are the lucky one. Living in this space is quite wonderful.

Wrath

Wrath is vengeful anger or retribution for an offense. It is used variously to describe the emotion of anger and the physical result of such anger. I've already talked in Chapter 1 about the colossal waste of time of carrying out, designing, or wishing for the punishment of others. Anger is always a response to perceived injustice. In the Bible, God's wrath is described as righteous because it is not based on the selfish desires of lust of the flesh, lust of the eyes, or pride but on an execution of justice. Man's wrath, as depicted in the Bible, is misplaced and comes from a desire to usurp God's authority as the dispenser of justice.[7]

Contrary to the biblical extreme, you know just from living life that, sometimes, the injustice perceived may also be quite real. You can be on the receiving end of unfair discrimination, pettiness, or jealousy. You can be accused of something you didn't do. You witness bullying or unfairness to another person. You witness a crime. If anger is a sin, then we are compelled to remain still and silent amidst such injustice. That's not patience; that's indifference.

Feeling anger is the proper response to injustice. It is right to be agitated—stirred—to action about that which we can change. Keep your emotions in the middle of the scale. Walk in patience always, but don't be afraid of anger. You will find balance.

Lust, gluttony, and sloth

These are habits resulting from wherever you reside on the self-esteem scale, and they show up in work and play. Laziness is considered a sin and diligence its opposing virtue. Yet we know that relaxation is an essential support to hard work. Imagine working at all times. Now imagine slacking (slothing) at all times. Not only are such extremes not good ideas; they are not sustainable. You can't work all the time, and you can't avoid work all the time. Rest makes work more productive, and work makes rest more enjoyable. Some of the best ideas materialize after we have exhausted the left hemisphere of the brain on the job, when the right hemisphere takes over while we're showering or sleeping.

In our play, namely sex and food, first we should be grateful that we live in a time and place where such activities can constitute play rather than means to our survival. We need food in order to live and sex to propagate our species, but we can enjoy both as pure pleasures of the human body. Food and sex are celebrations of life. That's why a meal is the main event when we recognize milestones—christenings, birthdays, graduations, weddings, and the like—and whenever families gather. Where we come from, alcohol is often a part of these gatherings. We celebrate with food and drink because we are happy to be alive, we are grateful for the love of our friends and family, and we rejoice in the special occasions that mark the journey of life. We celebrate with sex for similar reasons. We are happy to be alive, and we rejoice in our partner. Sex is the physical act of love, one of the highest expressions of love possible to human beings, because it engages our minds, bodies, and souls in absolute joy.

But food and sex are the ends, the culmination, of happiness, not the means to it. If you're not happy to be alive, and you don't recognize the love of friends, family, or your partner, no amount of food, alcohol, or sex will make these conditions so. Still, you've probably seen people who try to find fulfillment in promiscuity or large amounts of food or booze. To counteract and prevent such behavior, abstinence and chastity are offered as the opposing virtues to gluttony and lust. Replacing one extreme behavior with another doesn't bring balance, though.

Divide your behavior between making a life and enjoying life, between work and play. Let each refresh you and make you excited about the other. Too much play becomes addiction. Too much work becomes addiction too.

Self-esteem

Conceit — Pride — Humility — Shame

Giving

Greed — Earned — Generosity — Self-sacrifice

Emotions

Rage, Retribution — Anger — Patience — Indifference

Habits

Addiction — Work — Play — Addiction

The extreme ends of the scales, though opposites, are closer to each other than you might think. An extreme of haughty conceit often hides deep-seated feelings of shame from the opposite end of the scale. A display of self-sacrifice may be an attempt to assuage the guilt that can accompany greed. Indifference can hide a bottomless well of rage. And addiction develops at both extremes of the habits scale. It might be helpful to imagine the straight line of each scale as curved into a circle, with opposite ends meeting on the bottom of the circle. Balance on the top of that ball. It will tip to one side or the other with life's ups and downs. If you fall, getting back on top will require opening yourself to the suggestions in this book—help, reflection, and personal choices—and it all branches out from the self-esteem scale, the scale that reflects what you see as your worth.

I dreamed that the universe sent me a progress report. Down the left-hand side of the page, every realm in which I was attempting to grow was listed. Across the top of the page, three column headings read *Healed*, *In Progress*, and *Needs Work*, followed below by columns of open circles. The circles were filled in like this: *Healed*, two areas from the list. *Needs Work*, three areas from the list. In all other opportunities for growth, the *In Progress* circles were filled in. I think this is the progress report we should always expect and the way we should grade ourselves whenever necessary. We've accomplished some, and we've failed some, but mostly, we are learning. Place too many marks in the *Healed* column and your conceit points you toward a fall; too many in the *Needs Work* column and you risk becoming a victim. Maintain a balance, not only in your growth but in your evaluation of it.

In another dream, I made my way through a rainy, crowded city to the public bandstand, where I had previously placed piles of our clean, folded laundry. Only the top layer of laundry was wet from the rain, so it wasn't the total loss it could have been, but we had to figure out how to save the laundry and prevent the need to do it over. We knew we couldn't balance the piles of laundry if we attempted to carry them. So we donned all of the clothes simultaneously and wore them away from the bandstand. If dirty laundry is a metaphor for vice, then clean, folded laundry is a metaphor for virtue. Virtue is not for public display but to be worn like clothing. We can't carry it around like a parcel; we have to take it on. You can do it. Balance is beautiful.

Other People's Obsessions Are None of Your Business

I used to consider myself the most "live and let live" person in the world. As long as people didn't harm me, I was okay with whatever they did. I liked everyone…except liars, cheaters, criminals, bullies, losers, posers, narcissists, and the like. I'm sure you recognize this as another description of perfectionism, like in chapter 1. Perfection was my standard, and anything less was unacceptable. But I really didn't see it that way. I considered it a virtue that I never told anyone what to do. I was conceited in my judgment but humble in my non-delivery. I treated people the way I wanted to be treated, just like the golden rule says. I wanted to be left alone, and so I left people alone. I believed that you are what you do, that if you lie, you are a liar; if you cheat, you are a cheater. I equated people's behavior with who they are. This belief didn't leave any room for mistakes, my own or anyone else's.

The lesson came slowly and painfully. At first, I could make exceptions for people who truly couldn't control all their behavior—the sick, the schizophrenic, the downtrodden. I learned that everyone is going through something, and we may not know what it is. I understood that people's personal trauma could make them cranky and unlikeable. That was okay. I didn't have to be around any of them. They were like trees falling far off in the distance, where I couldn't hear them and could barely see. Then some trees fell on me.

Several of my loved ones, who are very good people, made some very big, bad choices. They destroyed families, friendships, and themselves. My philosophy could not encompass this. Believe me, my first reaction was to just cut them loose. Cut all ties. For the first time, my love for other persons came face-to-face with my own morality, and the two were not compatible. I had to choose between love and judgment. I had to decide who I was going to be—one who loves or one who judges. So far, it's the hardest thing I've ever done.

The Apostle Paul described love like this: "Love is patient, love is kind. It does not envy, it does not boast, it is not proud. It is not rude, it is not self-seeking, it is not easily angered, it keeps no record of wrongs. Love does not delight in evil but rejoices with the truth. It always protects, always trusts, always hopes, always perseveres. Love never fails."[8] I had heard those words a hundred times, mostly at weddings, and nodded in agreement, but I had never been tested in real life. I am none of these things if I abandon people. If I respond to others' desperate behavior with my own, I add to the darkness in the world. So now I choose to be one who loves.

What I had discounted in my prior thinking is that people don't do what they want to do, necessarily, but what they have to. They create and feed their own demons, and it is not for us to decide whether it is warranted. People deal with catastrophic loss—death, illness, and destruction. They deal with unspeakable abuse, neglect, and violence. That doesn't mean that lesser traumas are less traumatizing. The fear is real to the one who is afraid, regardless of our opinions about it. It doesn't matter whether the person is three years old or ninety-three or whether we find their suffering justified or not. We don't even have to decide if they're right or wrong. We don't have to judge other people's issues. We only have to be willing to open our hearts in the face of them—to anything and everything.[9] Whatever their obsession, it's none of our business.

Our business is love. I didn't have to look far for an example. The example comes from you. A mother's love for her child is the strongest and simplest love in the world—strong because nothing can break it, simple because it isn't learned or manufactured in some way. It just is. No matter what a child's behavior, that child is always loved. A mother doesn't stop loving her child when he misbehaves. She doesn't stop if he treats others badly. She doesn't stop, even if he robs, rapes, and murders. She abhors the behavior but never the child. She continues to love her child even as he screams "I hate you!" in her face. And, if she is able, she responds with even more love. This unconditional love is a great gift, not only to the child but to the mother. It's like the plants and the trees and all of nature being drawn toward the light. It could not be any other way.

I had to learn to expand this kind of love beyond my child, to see every human being as I see my child. I had to separate the idea of mother from the idea of love because it is not my place to mother anyone besides you (and occasionally your friend-siblings). I didn't want to be everyone's parent. But as this view of life materialized for me, I realized it was not mothering that I needed to expand—it was that strong and simple kind of love. This knowledge is a great relief to me, and it makes me wonder if I'm the only one who may have misunderstood. Maybe, in trying to understand unconditional love, somebody determined that God is a person and that God loves everyone as a parent loves his children. Maybe the parenting became equated with the love, so people formed religion and began to call him Father and Domino and Lord. What if God isn't Father or Lord of anybody? What if God is simply, yet profoundly, the wellspring of love?

When those you love become lost, their behavior is not who they are. If they become enveloped in darkness, they may not be able to produce anything but darkness. They may try to draw you into it, using your love as the tether. They may direct life-or-death, world-ending statements at you because their pain makes them believe their very life is at stake. Until they deal with their own pain, negativity will exude from them in all directions. See it for what it is, an outward expression of pain. It doesn't belong to you personally.

The lesson came slowly. But to be completely free, I also had to learn it painfully. Remember when I broke my back? You and your friend-siblings had T-shirts made that carried the hashtag "No patback" and an image of a hand within an international "no" sign. Those shirts were hilarious. And I am grateful to all the friends who brought food, ran errands, and did laundry for me when I couldn't move. Your own help was a lifesaver—placing me on the bed, dressing me, and generally tending to all needs below the knees since I could neither bend over nor reach that far. The whole experience was for me a humbling lesson in asking for help. Were that the only lesson, I would have placed this story in chapter 7, Ask for Help. But I believe that the overriding lesson taught by my debilitating injury belongs here. A friend who delivered dinner one evening put it into context for me. She must have been shocked at seeing my swollen, immobile body, which days before had been athletic and energetic. Her first words were, "What are you doing taking on other people's problems?"

Maybe it was a coincidence that the same friend had recently referred me to a psychic medium. Maybe not. I had received this prediction for a spirit-crushing loved one:

> He is about to get his candle snuffed out. Don't worry, it's not going to kill him. But he's not going to be able to move. He will need a great deal of help because he won't be able to do anything. I don't know exactly how it's going to go down. Let's say he falls down a flight of stairs or something and can't walk. Whatever amount of time they say it's going to take to heal, it's not going to take nearly that long. But he is going to need 24-hour care.

Two weeks later, I slipped and fell down the stairs while carrying a stepladder. Because I never let go of the ladder, I couldn't catch myself, and the full force of the fall landed me on the edge of a stair, breaking my L1, L2, and L3 transverse process bones. I had never broken a bone before that I remembered, so I was unprepared for the level of pain it could produce. I thought I could just stand, wait a few seconds, and move on. The pain raged in my back, as if I

38

were on fire. Still, I walked through the house, ever so slowly, to put the ladder away, and then climbed back up the stairs to call for help, your dog leaning against my leg with every agonizing step, as if she were trying to support my weight. Before my injury, I could bend over straight-legged and put my palms to the floor. After, I couldn't even bend my neck far enough to look at my toes. Despite the pain, I amazed the back doctor with my rate of healing, and I was able to bend over and touch my toes within six weeks, though he said it would probably take a year.

To sum up, I wasn't able to move. I needed a great deal of help because I wasn't able to do anything. I fell down a flight of stairs and couldn't walk. I needed twenty-four-hour care. And I healed in much less time than the doctor expected. Everything happened just as the medium had predicted, except it happened to me.

Even if you can't find anything to hold onto in this coincidence—as I myself am still grasping—you have to admit that the symbolism alone demonstrates the lesson. Did I somehow reach out into the universe and take on for myself the pain and injury that was meant for someone else? Is that even possible? I don't think it matters. Because even if I didn't do so with some sort of psychic energy or negative thought, I had been doing it in a more tangible way for most of my life. I doubt that symbolism alone would have so thoroughly convinced me to change. My back may have healed in record time because I was already healthy and physically fit. Or it could be that my back healed when, with love, I released another's problems back to him, when I learned that other people's obsessions are none of my business. It certainly felt that way.

You once said that what you hoped people would say about you is that you were always there for them. What I have just described is my path to the same. I hope to be secure enough to be there for my loved ones, no matter what their pain drives them to do. We may not be able to control the behavior of others, but we can be the light that shines into their world, a ray of hope, an example, and a source of endless love.

Suffering Is Optional

Loneliness is thirsty out at sea
And watching silent teardrops as they sink
With water for as far as eyes can see
But not a single drop that you can drink

Happiness is standing in the sun
With every new day drinking in the dew
And feeling as though life has just begun
And every single moment is for you

Perhaps someone has hurt you and hurt you so deeply you are amazed that you can still be alive. You're not the first person this has happened to, and you won't be the last. Here's what typically happens when someone experiences a great loss or series of losses: She cannot bear the loss. The pain is so raw and reaches so far that it threatens her very life. That's why it seems the world is at an end. So she represses the pain, buries it as deep as she possibly can. She builds a fortress around it so that nobody can ever find it, not even herself. And this seems to work. She spends time with people who appreciate her and pass the time in fun and entertaining ways. Over time, she learns that she can let a small number of these people in a little deeper, and their friendships grow closer. She goes off to college and finds the many skills and talents she possesses. She graduates, she finds a career, a husband who loves her. She reaches many milestones she expects will bring her happiness, and with each one, there is a nagging feeling of being let down. She ignores this and moves on.

But while she is building a life, the wound that she has buried is festering inside her. She is so good at keeping it out of her conscious mind that it finds other ways to come out. Maybe a physical pain or ailment of some kind. (If you cannot feel your emotions, if you are cut off from them, you will eventually experience them on a purely physical level, as a physical problem or symptom).[10] She goes to several doctors, but there isn't anything physically wrong with her that could be causing the symptoms. So she lives with chronic back pain or unexplained heartburn or sore throats that persist for weeks. Something. It becomes part of the regular course of her life. Those nagging feelings of being let down don't go away, and they always surface just as something great happens. This sets her sights on the pursuit of the next great thing even faster to make it go away. She becomes driven. And every once in a while, feelings of rage come out of nowhere, and she doesn't even know what she's angry about. Probably something that her husband said or did or something one of her children did. Her husband and her children are entirely innocent. They love her dearly. But she knows it isn't herself, so it must be their fault. Why can't they love her the way she wants to be loved? She begins to suspect that they don't actually love her, that they are causing her pain on purpose. She looks for confirmation of her fears and, of course, finds it. *She ignores any behavior that doesn't fit what she has decided is true and obsessively magnifies the smallest perceived slight.* She sets aside facts in favor of something more comfortable in the short term.

The stress of living with these people who don't even care about her grows rapidly now. So much is expected of her, and nothing is being returned. She finds it harder and harder to get through the day. She seeks something that helps to relieve the stress. Maybe it's alcohol or party drugs. Maybe she just likes to go to a bar and have men tell her she's pretty since her husband doesn't seem to appreciate her. Or maybe the drinking does the trick. Or maybe she throws herself into her job, working as much as she possibly can. Something.

Something that enables her to numb the pain. And she finds after some time that it's still not enough. It doesn't numb enough. So maybe the men's compliments turn into having affairs. Maybe the alcohol increases. Maybe the drugs. Maybe work becomes something she must do twenty-four seven. Whatever it is, now she is addicted to it and couldn't stop if she wanted to. She is indifferent to the pleas of her family members because she can't see that she has a problem. It is all their fault for not loving her. If only they would change, her life would improve. Her actions indelibly hurt the very people she is closest to. Without ever setting out to hurt others—in fact, setting out to *never* be like the person who hurt her, she has become exactly like him. She leaves her family and files for divorce. And though it is her own actions that created her dark situation, she feels nothing but anguish, as if the whole world has betrayed her. She feels that all those closest to her have hurt her, abandoned her, just as she knew they would. It is the original hurt all over again, magnified.

And the cycle begins again, with her own husband and children guarding their hearts and burying their hurt because they think they will die if they don't.

When we repress our emotions and bury our wounds so deep that even we ourselves can't find them, we end up designing our entire lives around avoiding that wound. At the same time that we congratulate ourselves for "not needing" the person who hurt us, everything we do is in search of the love we wanted from that person. Maybe that career isn't even the one we truly wanted, but the one that, on some level, we thought would make that person proud of us. That's why it's a letdown with every milestone—our behavior, no matter how noble and accomplished—can't control another person. Consequently, we don't feel fulfilled by the things in life that are supposed to fulfill us.

It is your choice whether to break this cycle. Suffering is optional. The wound in your heart will hurt like hell when you address it, but it will hurt only for a little while until you let it go. Then it can heal. And scar tissue tends to be much stronger than the original flesh. But an untended wound will fester and infect every aspect of your life. It can do this without you being consciously aware of it. So let it go, my dear. Let it go. It has nothing to do with you, with anything you do or did. You were just close at hand, is all. If the person who hurt you had someone else close at hand—someone not you—he would have done exactly the same thing. Because the thing that caused him to hurt you was not you. It was his own hurt. How you respond to it is entirely up to you. As soon as you know this in your heart—for real and not just as something you want to believe—you can let go. There are lots of professionals who can help you do this, along with family and friends you trust. But you can also do it by yourself. Yes, you are enough.

You are a being of light, the most beautiful thing you can imagine. As soon as you know this—for real—you can heal. More than that, you can help. Love truly is the answer. Begin by loving yourself enough to seek healing. I believe that everything that happens is for a reason. The negative things are not to make us suffer but to provide opportunities for growth.

I used to tell you when you were little that your job was "to play, to learn, and to grow." I said it to help you know your place in the world. I have come to believe that this is the same job we have into adulthood and for our entire time on this earth. Life is to be experienced. Learn from this one. And grow into the person you were meant to be. And play, if for no other reason than that it's fun.

When you read the sonnet that begins this chapter, note that the difference between loneliness and happiness is not what happens but one's stance toward it—in loneliness, thirsty and unfulfilled, in happiness, drinking in the day; in loneliness, watching life as if from outside it, in happiness, standing in full sun; in loneliness, alienated from the source, in happiness, as newly born. These are your alternatives. I choose to believe that the beautiful day is a gift to me, that the butterfly that follows me around is a spiritual hello from a friend who has passed, that rainbows are glimpses of the true beauty of everything.

On the night of your last high school softball game, I was treated to a vision like I have never before witnessed. You had already completed your graduation ceremony and hosted your graduation party, saying goodbye to your high school days. High school wouldn't *really* be over, though, until your softball team was shut out of the district tournament. A loss that night would represent the end of an era. And so it ended, in a respectable loss. After all the postgame hugs and tears, you climbed into the bus to ride home with the team, and the rest of us traveled in my car. We flew east down the highway, dodging intermittent showers, while behind us the sun was setting, and up ahead thunderstorms turned the sky black. Just as we were marking the end of your high school days and the new adventure awaiting you at college, a stunning rainbow painted the sky. I had seen many rainbows in my life, but none like this one. It was much brighter, more saturated with color, and the spectrum of light was more delineated than I knew was possible. Dark, thin bands were visible between the wide bands of bright colors. And there seemed to be an extra narrow band on each side, beyond the red and beyond the violet, repeating the full spectrum, like two mini-rainbows. Within minutes, another, less intense rainbow appeared. A faint third rainbow may have been visible for a few minutes. We weren't sure. All of this was against a black, not blue, sky, for the thunderstorms still raged far ahead of us. I happened to have my good camera along for photographing the game, so I pulled the car off to the side of the highway and took photographs. Before long, other cars pulled off the highway and spectators stood and pointed in awe. We commenced driving, exclaiming how none of us had ever seen such a beautiful rainbow. Were those extra color bands real or just an effect of the light? Isn't a rainbow itself just an effect of the light? Had anyone ever seen a rainbow against a black sky? We tried to figure it out. We kept exclaiming, "We're about to drive under it!" but we never did. The phenomenon lasted well over forty minutes. It was unique to all of our experience.

I choose to believe that that rainbow was a symbol of your bright future, a sign that we had done everything we could to prepare you for it. There is synchronicity in the fact that the three people in the car relate to you as mothers—Mom 2.0, your godmother, and me—that it occurred on just the right day and at the right time, that we were talking about you when it appeared. I can't think of a better metaphor for perspective because a rainbow doesn't exist at all, except when viewed from a certain coincidental perspective. Try as you might to travel under it or to find its end and bathe in its colors, your relationship to the water droplets and the light changes, and so does the perceived position of the rainbow.

I imagine the rainbow was a sign for others as well. A greeting from a loved one who had died recently, an idea for a creative artist, a burst of energy for a weary heart, a symbol of hope for someone in despair. But also, someone saw that awesome sight and cried tears of hopelessness, unable to imagine that life for them could ever be that beautiful. Because the difference between loneliness and happiness is not what happens, not the rainbow itself, but one's perspective—in loneliness, thirsty and unfulfilled, in happiness, drinking in the day; in loneliness, watching life as if from outside it, in happiness, standing in full sun; in loneliness, alienated from the source, in happiness, as newly born. So again I say: These are your alternatives.

There is nothing you need to do to care for your soul except to heed it. You have no other job besides living in accordance with it, embracing what fulfills it and saying no to what does not. As Michael Singer says, there is only one big spiritual decision you have to make in life. It's not whether you believe in God or which religion you commit to or which is the path to enlightenment. It's not even what your life's purpose is to be—that will manifest itself in time. It is whether you will be happy.[11] Whether you are looking for reasons to be depressed or reasons to be filled with joy, you will find them in abundance. Life throws a lot of crap at you. Pain is inevitable. Whether you hang on to it and feed it is a choice. You can choose to live in the light or live in darkness. That's it. Could it be that simple? Yes. It can also be just as difficult as you make it. Pain is inevitable. Suffering is optional.

Ask for Help

When you were three years old, you almost fell into the toilet. It was at Grandpa's house, and we had forgotten to bring the padded ring that converted the adult toilet seat into a toddler-sized one. In the space of a second, you felt yourself slip, called out, "Daddy, help me!" and he caught you before you could fall in. You were unharmed, and you seemed to forget about the incident as soon as it was over, with no lingering fear. That was it. I still marvel at the pure innocence of your experience. It signifies even more to me now. You did not weigh your value as a human being against the value of the help. You did not wait until you fell all the way in before you asked for help. You felt no guilt at having asked and no worry about asking in the future. You didn't need to learn how to ask. You didn't struggle with whom to ask nor anticipate the quality of their help but called out to one close to you. This is the simplicity with which we should ask for help.

First, you have to believe that you are worthy of help. You are. Can you think of one friend you would not help, if asked? Of course not. It is implicit in your friendship. Why should it be different the other way around? Denying those who love you the opportunity to help is to deny the bond between you, to separate them from you. It's an insult, like slapping your friendship in the face. Give your loved ones some credit. They will be there for you.

Second, you have to let go of any guilt or worry about asking. If you are afraid that asking for help will announce to the world that you are not perfect, well, the world already knows that. You might not want to admit it, but it's true. Nobody has ever been shocked that another person needed help. On the contrary, people are shocked when a person who *never* asked for help, a person who seemed to know all the answers and garner all the success in life, breaks down, turns to drugs or crime, or even suicide. Stress and negativity can build over a long period of time, but they can't go on forever. Ask for help sooner rather than later.

Third, asking for help doesn't require any special skills. "Help me" is all you need to know, and all you need to say. You've known how to do it your whole life. Ask for help and you will receive it. It's that simple.

But even when you ask for help, you have to be ready to accept it. To ask for help is to be ready to accept change. Ever since the Greek philosopher Heraclitus so accurately concluded that "change is the only constant," you would think people would act accordingly. But no, we resist it with committed rigidity. Keeping things the same is comfortable to us, even if "the same" is harmful and we know it. What a piece of work we are!¹²

Like weather, change is coming. Even with all our twenty-first-century meteorological technology, we can't predict the weather with much accuracy. And we can't control it. Some people complain constantly whenever the weather is not perfect (which is most of the time, where we come from). Or they waste all of autumn worrying about the winter to come. Others stay indoors to avoid bad weather. Some take a defiant stance: Bring on winter! I'm not even going to wear a coat. Take that! They raise a fist to the sky, suffer the freezing cold, but refuse to admit it. Still others only pretend to enjoy whatever the weather brings because it makes them appear superior to the complainers. A couple of your little cousins, when pelted with sudden hail, stood in the yard, yelling, "Ow! Ow! Ow!" because it just didn't occur to them to run for cover. So many contortions for something that's going to happen anyway. It would be much easier to open an umbrella when it rains or grab a coat when it's cold. I wonder if a correlation could be made between a person's stance toward the weather and his attitude toward life. How do you meet change?

To be receptive to change, your mind, heart, and even your body must be in the right position. Your mind is filled with more than just thoughts. It produces a running dialogue between you and yourself. You may hear this dialogue in the voices of your parents and peers. They probably use some of the same lines uttered by those who have made the greatest impressions on you, but that internal family, as Dr. Schwartz calls it, is of your own creation. You have been an interactive party in full-blown arguments among your internal family, arguments which consumed your attention and kept you from sleeping or from being aware of your waking moments. To be receptive to change, you have to step back from the dialogue. Decline to be drawn in. Your mind has to be quiet. Many people practice some form of focused mental energy to reach this state, such as meditation or prayer. So far, meditation hasn't worked for me. As soon as I quiet my mind, it travels to that ineffable place where creativity lives, and it usually returns with treasures—songs, ideas, moving messages. I enjoy these travels immensely, so I'm not inclined to try to stop them. Am I doing it wrong, or am I already reaching some greater realm? I don't know. It seems to me that prayer can be a gathering of thoughts, which are purposefully directed, or a practice of opening the mind and listening for guidance. And I'm not sure it matters how you quiet your mind, only that you do so.

To be receptive to change, your heart has to be open. While the internal dialogue of your mind is quiet, you might get a glimpse of the condition of your heart. Is it small and dark? Hungry? Injured? Bursting with joy? Without the constant comments from your mind, you can come up with the proper metaphor. You can tell if your heart is open by looking for two things—its willingness to give love and its willingness to accept love. My experience has taught me that you can give love without being able to accept it, at least to a certain extent, but you can't accept love without being able to give it. At least, I've never seen anyone who could accept love sincerely without the ability to return it. If you can't give love, is it because you fear being hurt? If you can't accept love, is it because you think you don't deserve it? To open your heart is to accept the risk of injury to it. It's your choice. When you decide that the rewards of an open heart are greater than the risk, you will make the right one.

To be receptive to change, even your body must be in the right position. This is what yoga is all about, despite its reputation in the West as a trendy form of exercise. Yoga has its roots in the training of mind and body together to dislodge the ego and expand consciousness. Yoga positions prepare your body for meditation and focus. A head bowed and hands folded in prayer serve the same purpose. Putting your body in a position that makes you receptive to change is what's important.

Even your everyday posture, from moment to moment, can make the difference between remaining closed and opening up to change. When your body is misaligned, hunched, or in other ways set against the world, it sends signals to your brain that you are in distress. Stress hormones, like adrenaline, norepinephrine, and cortisol flood your system. A constant diet of stress hormones weakens your immune system, raises your blood pressure and blood sugar, leads to obesity, worsens depression, and causes a host of other health issues. Pain becomes chronic. Dr. Pete Egoscue has developed a method of placing the body in balanced posture to relieve pain, often instantly (The Egoscue Method). He believes that "often, troubling health issues are centered in the emotions rather than in any internal, physical malfunction or shortcoming."[13] In his clinics, he sees patients so rigidly opposed to change that they endure constant physical pain, stiffly running, stiffly inline skating and golfing, stiffly playing a variety of weekend sports because the facts say they have to keep fit,[14] when their issue isn't lack of exercise but a refusal to look inward. Our bodies can help our minds and hearts prepare for change.

Sometimes, we are so braced against change that it takes a disastrous loss—something that convinces us the world is ending—to sufficiently upset the positioning of our minds, hearts, and bodies. If this occurs, as you grieve the loss, quiet your mind, open your heart, and attune your body. It takes time, a different amount of time for each person. You will survive. You can thrive.

Vous Etes Votre Seule Limite

T wo people lived in a virtual paradise, focused in the moment, neither worrying about the future nor the past. All they needed was provided for them. Their lives were a lot like our own dog's life. Look at her. Her needs are few—food, exercise, and some petting. She doesn't contemplate her own mortality, nor set goals, nor make wishes, nor question her own actions. She is content. More than that, she is certain. It might be better to say that because she is certain, she is content. Has she ever made a decision that she regretted for more than one second? Even when she absconded with a stolen mouthful of detergent from the dishwasher, she never gave it another thought. She is without a human internal monologue that tells her she is wrong or inadequate. She shows all emotions sincerely and fully, without second-guessing herself. Her state of contentment and certainty is unrelated to her level of intelligence or physical abilities. Like all the animals, she knows her place in the world.

So these two people lived in a similar way, in contentment and certainty, until the day when they ate the fruit of a certain forbidden tree. Though they had been told this action would result in their doom, they did it anyway. Perhaps they were simply more curious than a typical house dog, and they couldn't help themselves. But it really doesn't matter—in literature's most beautiful vortex of irony, the couple in this story couldn't have grasped the consequences of their action until after the action was taken.

With the ingestion of the forbidden fruit came the knowledge of their own mortality, accompanied by a nascent sense of dissatisfaction. Living in the moment became lost to fear and worry about the past and future. They acquired a rational mind and became conceptual-thinking beings. They acquired a discernment of good and evil and became moral beings. They sought productivity and knew they would now labor for their sustenance.[15] There was no more dog's life, for they had traded certainty for the duality of the human condition. In Taoism, it is the yin and the yang. To ancient Greek philosophers, it was the Unity of Opposites. A more recent metaphor poses two wolves fighting within each of us.[16]

Biblical scholars are divided as to whether knowledge from the "tree of knowledge"[17] refers to omniscience, moral discernment, divine wisdom, or sexual desire.[18] Everyone else seems to be divided as to whether this knowledge is the scourge or the salvation of mankind. Whether curse or virtue, we comprise all these things. We are creatures of mind and productivity. With knowledge of our mortality, we can choose our morality and our sexuality. Even if we could manage to deny most of that, we can't unknow our own mortality. Your choice may seem to be either/or: Either you live in contentment and ignorance or as a conceptual and dissatisfied being; either you live like the couple before they ate the fruit or are fated to discontent; either happy or smart. I don't think so.

Imagine the couple in the garden as they changed. Their first feeling was fear as their inner struggles commenced. Their first judgment, once they discerned good from evil, must have been against themselves. They had disobeyed, made a mistake. Suddenly, they felt ashamed. They reproached themselves and hid their bodies with clothes, a metaphor showing the disguises and masks behind which we hide our real selves. So the inner dialogue began. When questioned, their first inclination was to judge and blame someone else for their own behavior. Their far-reaching minds allowed them to imagine the future and to begin to plan for it but also to fear it. Conceptual thought enabled their species to build skyscrapers and rocket to the moon. It also allowed for every terror and catastrophe to be conceivable. Their high-powered brains enabled them to analyze the past and learn from their mistakes. It also invited guilt, worry, and shame. Having to labor for their sustenance ended their leisurely lifestyle but also inspired the most creative production since the planet itself. Yin and yang. The Unity of Opposites. Two wolves. Virtue and vice. One can become the other so easily.

The doom about which the couple was warned, the source of all discontent and despair, the origin of conflict, suffering, and misery, is the struggle between these two extremes. It's you fighting with yourself.

Instead of accepting life as it unfolds, we insist on controlling it. And when life doesn't go our way, we suffer anxiety. We complain, "Unfair!" and "Why me?" and confirm to ourselves that we are not adequate for the task of pressing our will upon the world. Well, of course, we're not. When it comes right down to it, we can't control anything but our own behavior. But instead of accepting what we can't control, we pick ourselves up, reinflate ourselves with determination and hope, and try again—only to be defeated again sometime in the future. Adam and Eve's mistake was not that they disobeyed God, but that they tried to *be* God.

They traded living as creatures in harmony with their world for seeking to master the world. A master, by definition, is one having control. In verb form, to master something is to have full knowledge of it. Look up the word *master* in the dictionary—all the origins point to *knowing*. Look up the word *know*, and you will eventually find *apprehend* (to seize or grasp, as fruit from a tree) and to anticipate, especially with anxiety, fear, or dread. In the depths of our own language, we have equated knowledge with dread. And the fear and dread of our own deaths makes us desperate to maintain control over what we cannot. In another swirling irony—this one in the human soul—the only way to dispel the fear is to relinquish control, and relinquishing control can be the scariest thing we do. If there is a secret to life, this is it.

A lot of people are doing a lot of trying. They're trying to break habits, adopt new ones, lose weight, quit smoking, reduce stress, be kinder, and so forth. The trying is an indication of the internal struggle. If we could make some peace with ourselves, parts of us would not work actively against other parts, and we wouldn't have to *try* at all. We would simply do. I agree with Yoda's imperative to Luke Skywalker: "Always with you what cannot be done. Hear you nothing that I say?… You must unlearn what you have learned… Try not. Do. Or do not. There is no try."[19] Whenever you hear yourself telling someone what you are trying to do, it reveals a struggle. Step back and observe the fight, but don't get involved. Changing from the outside in does not address the internal struggle, and the changes must be monitored constantly. They're not permanent. Changing from the inside out resolves the internal struggle so that the outside takes care of itself. To say it another way, changing from the outside in works on the behaviors that result from the internal struggle while changing from the inside out eliminates the desire for those behaviors. It can happen, literally, overnight. I know because that's how it worked for me. This is liberation. Stop the fight. Let it dwindle and die. Surrender.

The Alcoholics Anonymous organization has been implementing the surrender of control since its inception in the 1930s. It is Step Three of the AA twelve-step program: "Made a decision to turn our will and our lives over to the care of God as we understood him." It's not intended to be a religious commitment, necessarily, but a reliance on a power greater than oneself (after becoming aware of that power in Step Two). Step Three changed my life, and it can change yours too.

Many coincidences converged to lead me to AA—research for a piece of fiction I was writing, a book I read that led to another book and another, a phone call from a friend, a dream about flying with the wind rather than against it. That line from my former employer about being the most alcoholic personality found its way to the surface of my mind. As bizarre as it seems, messages from a beloved relative—one spoken to me in a dream and one through a spiritual medium—were quotes straight from AA literature I hadn't read yet. It was as if everything in my world was pointing me in the same direction. As I read about black and white thinking, perfectionism, and sensitivity, I realized I was reading about myself. Chuck C. says that all alcoholics share three traits. First, every alcoholic is a perfectionist. Perfectionism makes us set goals for ourselves that we cannot attain, and we're forever disappointed in our performance. Second, we were born with the interior awareness that life should be a good and a big and a beautiful thing. Third, we are a highly sensitive people with a great capacity for feeling. He is convinced that these traits are the characteristics for alcoholism, except for alcohol. "This is our problem," he says, "a basic spiritual unrest."[20]

Note that all this is even before alcohol is added. I couldn't have found a better description of myself. Can you see the blurry mix of conceit and humility that flows into and out of such a personality? Nothing was ever good enough for me, most especially myself. Simultaneously, I tasked myself, alone, with changing a disappointing world into something beautiful. And I tortured myself for not being able to do it. I sensed that my emotions ran deeper than those of other people, and I bore this as the suffering that the world demands of a creative artist. Spiritual unrest, indeed.

Alcoholics are the people who battle this spiritual unrest with alcohol. What about the rest of us? For this isn't the condition of just one segment of society but the human condition. Here's what I did: I began to work the steps myself. When I got to Step Three, I didn't even know to whom I should address my surrender. I called on my "Personal God," whatever that might be, the Greatest Good of the Universe, the Spirit of Love, an Idea of Light and Anyone Who Can Help Me. And then I gave up. I surrendered my will to something greater.

I don't recall the date that I began, but I can tell you what the world looked like from one day to the next. The difference is stark because I happened to be in the same physical location two evenings in a row. The first night, or I should say the last night of my former outlook, I went to the monthly jam session down at the KC Hall. Friends and musicians of all ages gathered to play and sing the old songs, what used to be called country and western music. I had avoided the jam for months because the music—any kind of music—was like salt to the wounds I was harboring. In my emotional state at the time, I thought I might be able to attend as part of the audience, even if my heart wasn't ready to let me sing or play.

The Knights of Columbus Hall is like many historical buildings in the Midwest, once grand and stately, modernized in the 1970s by replacing the grandeur with faux bois paneling and fuel-efficient dropped ceilings and neither restored nor modernized again, ever after. I looked around the room, at the shabby walls and feeble attempt at trim, and fell into 1979. I was eighteen years old, excited to walk into a venue where I might get a chance to take the stage and sing. I had saved up for a year to buy a white fur jacket to seal my image as a performer who was headed somewhere, somewhere far better than the cornfields of Middle America. The funny thing is, I don't even remember whether I sang that night. I don't remember the audience. I don't remember why, at that age, I entered the building alone. I remember only the shabby walls, the feeble attempt at trim. Swirl-textured drywall. Hollow doors that failed to block the freezing December wind. And my white fur jacket. And the feeling that life was never going to be as good as I expected it to be.

The KC Hall took me right back to that time and reminded me that despite all of my travels and life experiences, despite all I had accomplished, I was right back in a cold, crappy building in the Midwest, accompanied by the very same songs from that earlier era. Disappointed. I had gone nowhere.

I was chatting with some friends about our respective backgrounds and parents while the music at the KC Hall twanged on. When I pulled up my parents' wedding photo on my phone to show the group, and comments on their good looks commenced, I inexplicably burst into tears. I spent the next thirty minutes in the restroom trying to compose myself. Then I ducked out of the building without talking to anyone.

The second night, or I should say the first night of my new outlook, I was back at the KC Hall, this time as a volunteer, serving food to the community at a fundraising event. I greeted the diners warmly and asked about their day. I had a lovely conversation with a small girl about the button missing from her coat and how she hoped Santa would bring her a new one for Christmas. I made a mental note to be on the lookout for a large purple button. For picky customers, I made special exceptions to the portion guidelines. They liked that.

I boxed extra food for parents with teenagers at home. The seventies-era decor was warm and charming then. The building seemed like a nostalgic embrace of the people inside it. And I marveled that it was the very same place I had despised the night before. I pulled up the picture of my parents again, just to pinch myself, make sure all this was real. I thought, *Yes, they are very good-looking* and smiled to myself. Nothing in that building had changed from one night to the next, except for something inside of me.

If you are looking for the real source of despair, suffering, and misery, it is the same for you as for everyone. It's you fighting with yourself, and you always lose in that fight. You might think that the smarter you are, the easier it should be to give it up. But that's not so. Imagine two boxing matches—one between supercut, heavyweight muscle men and the other between a couple of lightweight, scrawny weaklings. Both fights are evenly matched so that neither fighter in the respective contests can ever win. In which bout will the most damage be done? It will be the one in which the fighters have more resources with which to fight. Being the intellectual equivalent of the heavyweights doesn't make you immune. It probably makes it worse, as you have greater resources and higher expectations. Nobody ever wins this battle.

Give it up. Stop trying to control something you never had control of anyway. You are your own limit.

Mind Why

Your cousin, Buddy, is one of those super high energy people who ask a ton of questions and listen intently, as if whatever you are saying about any subject is fascinating. I have seen him coax laughter from the soberest people, vulnerability from the guarded, and hugs and I-love-yous from those who otherwise never engage in affection. I tried his technique years ago on a surly Walmart checker. She was clearly in a bad mood and, with no provocation from me, seemed determined to ruin my day by being rude. I knew what to do. I would turn her frown upside down. And I knew how to do it too. I had seen Buddy do it a thousand times. I would take a nonthreatening stance, ask about her day, and nice her to death, or at least to the point of smiling. After what seemed like a half hour (it was probably about three minutes in reality), finally, she did smile. I wished her a great day and took my packages out to the car. Any positive feelings of goodness or accomplishment on my part, though, were shadowed by utter exhaustion. I was uncertain if I could muster the energy to complete the rest of my errands for the day. I really needed to take a nap. If such encounters required that kind of mental and physical energy, I decided I would rather not take up the challenge. We can spend our lives like this—doing *what* we've been told is the right thing and even knowing *how* to do it—and exhausting ourselves in the process, if we don't mind *why*.

If I encountered that same store checker today, the positive energy radiating from me would do most of the work of lifting her spirit. It wouldn't deplete my own energy because it already flows through me. I don't have to muster it from nothing. I am more attuned to why. I have a different relationship to other people. I am connected. Talking to other people is no longer a chore but a regular part of my day. There goes me. I am talking to myself, and it's easy.

You might see me pause for a few moments before I eat a meal, looking like I am praying. You could call it that. Long ago, my mother and the church gave me the *what* and the *how*, with "Bless us, oh Lord, and these, Thy gifts, which we are about to receive, from Thy bounty, through Christ, our Lord. Amen." Despite that the ritual of prayer before meals dates back to ancient times, that my most cherished friends practice it, and even despite that the reason for the prayer is contained within it (that the food we eat is a gift), it wasn't until I discovered the *why* for myself that it made sense. At the very least, a pause to consider what we put in our bodies and to accept it with gratitude brings us to the present moment, which I described in chapter 2 as the best place—I mean, time—to be. Saying "I am grateful for this food and the nourishment it will bring my body," which is what I say, supplies positive energy to the act of eating. Gratitude affects brain waves for the better.[21] Positive words assist in proper digestion.[22] Making reference to nourishment gives me a moment to reconsider any *non*nourishing food choices I may have made before the food goes in. The world becomes brighter for a moment every time I mind why and put voice to gratitude.

Here's another example: The acts of saying please and thank you are pretty obvious as the right things to do. And we certainly know how to do them. But the *why* makes an enormous difference. Every sincere please or thank you, with reasons behind it, brings light into the world. It confirms to people that they are respected and that their actions are appreciated. Being that light is its own reward.

Whenever I hear my mind offer a comment that begins with "I don't have to…," I recognize it as a negative resistance. I don't have to put money in the bell ringer's bucket. I don't have to say an additional thank-you to someone I have already paid with a service or cash. I don't have to recognize other people's preferences, tolerate their quirks, or empathize with their needs. I thank my mind for commenting and proceed to do whatever it is I don't have to. I do these things, not because I am looking for anything in return, and not even because they are the right things to do, but because I am a golden ray of light that seeks itself in others. It is who I am. You, too, are a being of light. You can make the world a better place, constantly, without diminishing yourself.

To mind why is to listen to your own mind conversations without being a party to them. Become self-aware. Would it kill you to be kind? Would it exhaust you? If so, then you are not minding why; you are ignoring why.

I made some monumental vows when I was very little: "I will never be angry like my mother" and "If I am good enough, I will earn the love I need." In practice, these decisions didn't turn out to be beneficial for me. I carried anger around in my own invisible baggage for half a century. I collected it. I thought it never showed. As for the "good enough" vow, I made myself responsible for pretty much everything that occurred in my life. Events beyond my control were nonetheless my fault.

You, too, probably made at least one decision before the age of five that you have always lived by. Think about that. At your age, and for your whole life, you've been taking the advice of a toddler. Chances are, your decision was way off base and somehow related to ways in which you felt hurt. If you are experiencing emotional pain right now, it is probably not the first time. You may not remember the early childhood experiences, but your heart stored the feelings associated with them. You didn't have the intellectual capacity at that age to process your emotions. This is part of the human experience and entirely normal. Often the event that caused you pain was simply something you misunderstood because you were, like, two. Now that you do have the intellectual capacity to process your emotions, the memories likely have faded, but whenever you suffer a similar experience, the familiar emotions come flooding back. A sure indicator of this is when you actually feel like a small child for some unknown reason.

I am entirely unaware of the reason I felt my mother had abandoned me when I was three or four. I was at my grandmother's house, a safe and wonderful place where I spent much of my time as a child, awaiting Mother's return from some errand or meeting. I stood at the living room window watching the road, my forehead pressed to the glass and my hands balled together in the corner of the windowsill. I was so small. But I was acutely aware of the feelings of abandonment. I was suddenly and absolutely certain that she was never coming back, ever. It was as though a vice were squeezing my heart into a tiny stone. Surrounding the tiny stone, a hollow emptiness erased my being. I was ceasing to exist. I was unaware also why I did not go to my grandmother for comfort or to tell her that I thought I was dying.

I wanted that one person, not a hundred others. I would express the same sentiment when a first-grade boy rejected my profession of love on the playground and again when my twenty-year-old live-in boyfriend packed up and left the state while I was out to dinner with friends. I would express the same sentiment yet two more times in my life before I learned. "Mind Why" doesn't mean asking why those other people kept abandoning me but asking why I attached myself to people who tended to cut and run. Add the two life decisions I made as a child—I made them leave because I wasn't good enough, and I won't show any anger about it—and you've got a recipe for victimhood. I needed to learn that it's shame and fear that make people run, and I had to become more understanding of others' mistakes. Life gives us so many opportunities to learn. We need only take them. Sometimes it takes a lot of opportunities before the lesson is ultimately learned. Take them, my dear. When you are scared, it means you are about to learn something. "Mind Why".

Sources, Resources, The Source

The titles for the chapters in this book came from diverse sources. "Mind Why" was delivered to me in a dream years ago, but I did not understand it until recently. "*Vous Etes Votre Seule Limite*" is something I saw on a high fashion French T-shirt. "Other People's Obsessions Are None of Your Business" is adapted from a common saying in Alcoholics Anonymous. It's also something your grandpa often reminds me. "Suffering Is Optional" is pervasive wisdom in the fields of psychology, past-life regression therapy, Eastern and Western religions and philosophy, and health. I read piles of books in those areas in preparation for this writing. They are my external sources. I also used internal sources—enlightened perception and awareness, experiments in focus and living in the now. Anything can be a source for learning and wonder.

Moriah Rhame (a.k.a. Moriah the Medium) has been a life-altering source. Through her rare gift, I was able to speak with, or perhaps exchange energies with, Grandpa, his grandmother, my grandparents, my mother, and the man who lived in our house half a century ago. Was it some kind of trick? I don't think so, since Moriah had no prior information about me. She didn't even know my name. A couple of people who came through during the session had died long before I was born. Just the possibility that we have cheerleaders in the spirit realm, sending positive support, is enough to send my own spirit soaring. Here's what I take away from my experience with Moriah: When we leave this world, there is little that we take with us. We can't take our work even though we spend most of our lives entrenched in it. That's quite naturally human but not spiritual. We can't take money or possessions as much as we are attached to them and enjoy them on earth. We can't take our reputations. We can't take our good looks or bodies. We *can* take what we have learned and our relationships with people. I don't think there is an omnipotent being who passes judgment on us and metes out reward and punishment. I think the judge of how you have lived your life is yourself—yourself from whatever enlightened perspective you gain when you move into another state of existence. I believe it's an eternal, universal perspective. Your grandmother, who, in life, was complicated and difficult, has, in death, decided to remain on this earth to help you because her spirit loves you so much. Now *that's* what I call an enlightened new perspective! If you remind yourself of all the people who support and encourage you, including ones who have passed, you will walk on a cloud, light as air. You are so loved.

I have found something. It seems to be something *out there* and also something inside myself. And they are connected, symbiotic. It is a source of peace, for I feel at peace. It is a source of boundless energy, for I now have energy to spare. It has lifted an unbearable weight from my spirit, making everything I do in my daily life easier. It is the absence of fear, worry, guilt, and need. It is a source of awe, wonder, and gratitude. The sky is bluer; the sun brighter. I recognize the lifelong fight with myself for what it is, so it can be over. The spiritual call it The Ultimate Source; the religious, God; holistic healers, the Universal Life Force Energy. In Chinese medicine, it is chi. In the Japanese tradition, it is known as Reiki. George Lucas calls it the Force. Call it anything you like.

With this something comes the ability to enjoy each moment, turning time from my adversary into my friend, giving me millions of *nows*. Living in an infinite now is an amazing gift. I have lost interest in judging other people by my own rigid standards. Frequently, I am so appreciative for random sensory experiences that the world seems made expressly for me. The joy and awe of existing as a human being is available to everyone. The source is unlimited, and it is both within you and hanging invisibly in the ether, as accessible as radio waves or light. "Think of what your life might be like if all the energy you spent, for example, angrily stewing about what others have done to you or obsessively daydreaming about your missing soul mate, was available to you in the present moment and was channeled toward fully enjoying whatever you were doing now. What if the strength of your urge to binge became a confidence and focus that helped you connect with people?"[23]

I am tempted now to describe the amazing connectedness I feel to other people, to nature, and to the cosmos. But I think this is something you can experience for yourself. Words would defy the truth of personal experience. I am most amazed, and continually amazed, at the effect of this *something* on practical, everyday activities, no matter how small. I love changing light bulbs and sweeping the garage floor and cooking dinner. I love when the snow falls and when it rains, when the sun rises over the river and when it sinks behind the hill. I can enjoy your competitive sporting events without stressing over the outcome. I can drive down the hill of Third Street without fear that the leaning trees will fall on me. I can stand outdoors in a thunderstorm without fear that lightning will strike me. I don't feel the pressing need to be right. I can sing for an audience without stage fright. I can write freely. I joke around with my internal critic. I can express love with no reservations. I have said, "I love you" more times in the past year than in my whole life before that. Sometimes I literally jump into the air with the excitement of being alive.

I don't know how this *something* operates nor why. But the more I practice attention and let life happen, the more connections form. It emanates from me and from others at the same time and seems to be swirling in and around everything. My friend LuAnn calls the messages from it "God whispers"[24] and she has made listening and acting upon them her life's work. One summer night, as we sat outside talking about this very subject, dusk settled across the yard. Yet she remained in a soft glow. I thought maybe it was a trick of the twilight or a result of my gratitude for her friendship, but she suddenly appeared to be the most beautiful woman I had ever seen. Some would call it her aura, others, the Holy Spirit shining through her, and still others, the light of a heavenly angel. I know only that it was an uplifting and positive experience, beyond any need to figure it out. I didn't remark on it. I simply reveled in it. I wonder if it is possible to enjoy that kind of vision permanently. And I believe that, somewhere inside, we all are that beautiful.

Science offers no satisfactory explanation for this kind of energy. Physics tells us that everything is energy and that energy is indestructible. Yet much of the energy in the universe is unaccounted for by our current mathematics. If I have encountered but a tiny slice of it, imagine how much more there must be. We have a mortal physical body and a marvelous computer of a brain. We have consciousness, which is not yet understood. You can read *Consciousness and the Universe* if you are looking for what the *Journal of Cosmology* has published on the subject.[25] I spent a whole summer reading those scientific papers, looking for answers. And you can read Dr. Elisabeth Kubler-Ross's extensive research in the existence of consciousness beyond the physical body.[26] Ervin Laszlo presents "some of the truly credible and robust strands of the evidence" in *The Immortal Mind.*[27] We haven't been able to measure consciousness because it isn't a physical phenomenon; it's metaphysical. We can't even find it, let alone quantify it, yet we know it exists. Consciousness is where the mystery of life resides. It may be from whence the *something* I've found arises. Remain open to it. You are a part of it. "It doesn't matter if you believe in God, angels, spirit guides, or not. You are from the same strand of light that connects you to the universe, and every being to the beginning of time... You are a part of the universe. You are your God source, angel, and guide. You are a part of the whole."[28] As you discover who you are, look beneath the noise of your mind and past any pain in your heart. Go to the source. It's you.

The Message Is Love and the Secret of Snow

thought the world was ending. I had nowhere to turn. For so long, I had relied on only myself to the extent that even if I were to ask for help, I didn't know to whom to address that plea. Call it a prayer. Anne Lamott says there are three essential prayers—help, thanks, and wow.[29] Thanks and wow wouldn't come to me for a while, and I didn't even know if I was worthy of help. Call it an experiment of consciousness. What if I simply asked for a message, any message, and let any power of the universe deliver it. So I did. I lay my head down to sleep, only to awaken hours later, sitting up suddenly, with these words, loud, clear, and filling my head: *The message is love.*

From that moment on, in what is the most awe-inspiring phenomenon I've ever experienced, I was assisted in learning the meaning of the message. People, books, dreams, adventures, and everyday experiences seemed to appear from every corner and converge into one constant. Were they sent to me? Did I summon them? How could everything in my world be made just for me and everything in yours also be made for you? Eckhart Tolle says that "life will give you whatever experience is most helpful for the evolution of your consciousness. How do you know this is the experience you need? Because this is the experience you are having at the moment."[30] For me, I know only enough to know that I don't know. What I've been telling you is the route that got me here. Now that I understand the message, I want to pass it on to you.

Tend the negative because you created it in fear as a shield against hurt. Carefully and lovingly remove the steel from around your heart so it can fulfill its purpose. Your weakness will become your strength.

Practice attention because in doing so, you will become fulfilled. Be present in every moment that you can. Giving your attention will become all the attention you need.

Speak up, no matter what, because the alternative is regret.

Seek balance because in balance, there is peace. Extremes will fall away without a struggle because you really don't need them.

Other people's obsessions are none of your business. You would likely behave the same way in their shoes. Let them come to the light for themselves. Don't judge. Be there for them.

Pain is inevitable. Suffering is optional. Choose joy.

Ask for help because you were never meant to be alone in the world. Ready yourself for change if change is needed. Your loved ones will be there for you. I will always be there for you.

You are your own limit. Stop fighting that losing battle and enjoy the experiences of life rather than trying to rearrange and control them.

Mind why because it's the door to enlightenment and joy. We become ourselves by being the observer of ourselves. We care for our souls by heeding them.

Be open to the sources of enlightenment and enjoy the energy that comes with the openness.

Remember that you are loved. Here is the message: Even if you fail at everything in this book or choose to ignore it, still you are loved. No matter how far you fall from perfect, no matter how bad your decisions, still you are loved. No matter what your inner struggles, still you are loved. If you are lost, still you are loved. Still and still, you are loved.

We grow our own troubles, just like snowfalls pile up and grow to cover mountains. They seem dense and impenetrable and make us so unbelievably cold. I want to send you the message now, before the snow has a chance to become deep. But even if it does, know the secret of snow. It is practically nothing at all. It is a bit of water, a teardrop that turned cold and crystalized. It couldn't have survived in the first place without attracting more of itself. And as simple as that, it will melt in the warmth of your hand and disappear in the light of your heart.

AFTERWORD

I will read any book that a friend recommends to me. My hope is that in doing so, I will learn something more about that friend and that we will draw closer. It might even be a good book. As for online book reviews, I usually stay away from them because I want to form my own opinions about what I read. With surprise, late one night, I found myself poring over the reviews of a book that Amazon thought I would like. I don't take Amazon's recommendations nearly as seriously as those from friends. Yet there I was, deep in analysis mode, several hours passing before I again became aware of time. What intrigued me so was the fact that of the hundreds of reviews, only a handful gave the book two or three stars. The overwhelming majority gave one star or five stars, claiming the book was either the worst or the best book the purchaser had ever read.

Every book speaks in a certain tone, and that tone strikes different people differently. You found this book helpful, or you did not. But the fact that you read it shows you are looking for something. If you didn't find it here, don't stop looking. Many authors say essentially the same thing. Keep listening until one's voice is music to your ears.

NOTES

1 Lynnclaire Dennis, *The Pattern*. (Lower Lake: Integral Publishing, 1997).

2 Richard C. Schwartz, PhD, *Introduction to the Internal Family Systems Model* (Oak Park: Trailheads Publications, 2001). I wrote, "So I'm not crazy" in the margin. Is it a coincidence that, in writing my novel, I divided my own internal family into three separate characters, living within one person? I think not. Dr. Schwartz's method confirmed what I could describe lyrically, but not yet formulate logically.

3 Victor E. Frankl, *Man's Search for Meaning* (Boston: Beacon Press, 1959).

4 Charles A. Chamberlain (a.k.a. Chuck "C"), *A New Pair of Glasses* (Irvine: New Look Publishing Company, 1984).

5 Ayn Rand., *The Ayn Rand Lexicon*. Ed. Harry Binswanger (New York: Penguin Books, 1986).

6 Jack Wellman, "What is the Biblical Definition of Pride? How is Pride Described in the Bible?," n.p. [cited Dec 7, 2018]. Online: https://www.patheos.com/blogs/christiancrier/2015/05/22/what-is-the-biblical-definition-of-pride-how-is-pride-described-in-the-bible/

7 Michael L. Williams, "How Does the Bible Define the Term Wrath?," n.p. [cited Dec 7, 2018]. Online: https://www.whatchristianswanttoknow.com/how-does-the-bible-define-the-term-wrath/#ixzz5Z2J4WMlG

8 Corinthians 13:4–8a

9 Michael A. Singer, *The Untethered Soul: The Journey Beyond Yourself* (Oakland: New Harbinger Publications, Inc., 2007).

10 Eckhart Tolle, *Practicing the Power of Now* (Novato: New World Library, 1999). Other noted authors align with Eckhart on this. Read *You Can Heal Your Life* and *Heal Your Body* by Louise Hay, *Feelings Buried Alive Never Die...* by Karol K. Truman, *The Body Keeps the Score* by Bessel van der Kolk M.D.

11 Michael A. Singer, *The Untethered Soul: The Journey Beyond Yourself* (Oakland: New Harbinger Publications, Inc., 2007). This is the same thing Singer says, colored by my own experience and words.

12 William Shakespeare, *Hamlet*, Act II, Scene 2, Prince Hamlet's soliloquy to Rosencrantz and Guildenstern, "What a piece of work is a man! How noble in reason, how infinite in faculty! In form and moving how express and admirable!

In action how like an angel, in apprehension how like a god!" Shakespeare knew.

13 Pete Egoscue, *Pain Free Living* (New York: Sterling Ethos, 2011).

14 Pete Egoscue.

15 Ayn Rand, *Atlas Shrugged* (Random House, New York: 1957), Galt's speech.

16 This is a fairly recent (21st century) bit of wisdom attributed to Cherokee legend. It is said that a young boy asks his grandfather, "Which wolf wins?" to which the grandfather replies, "Whichever one you feed."

17 Let's use today's vocabulary—the "Tree of Ego."

18 Kyle Greenwood, "Tree of Knowledge," n.p. [cited Oct 3, 2018], Online: https://www.bibleodyssey.org/en/passages/related-articles/tree-of-knowledge.

19 George Lucas, *Star Wars: Episode V—The Empire Strikes Back*. Hamill, Mark, Harrison Ford, and Carrie Fisher. 20th Century Fox, 1980. Yoda instructs the young Jedi to stop fighting with himself.

20 Charles A. Chamberlain (a.k.a. Chuck "C"), *A New Pair of Glasses*, (Irvine: New Look Publishing Company, 1984). Paraphrased from p. 134–137.

21 Alex Korb, PhD and Daniel J. Siegel, MD, *The Upward Spiral: Using Neuroscience to Reverse the Course of Depression, One Small Change at a Time* (Oakland: New Harbinger Publications, 2015). The authors demonstrate that even the mental search for things to be grateful for, whether you find any or not, creates a positive effect on the brain.

22 Adelle Davis, *Let's Cook It Right* (New York: Harcourt, Brace and Company, 1947). There is so much more to food than strikes the tastebuds. You won't see a recipe in this old cookbook until the end of chapter 7.

23 Richard C. Schwartz, PhD, *Introduction to the Internal Family Systems Model* (Oak Park: Trailheads Publications, 2001).

24 LuAnn Anderson, *God Whispers*. Not yet published, but available soon. I am honored to call her my friend.

25 Sir Roger Penrose, Stuart Hameroff, MD, and Subhash Kak, PhD, eds. *Consciousness and the Universe: Quantum Physics, Evolution, Brain & Mind* (Cambridge: Journal of Cosmology, Cosmology Science Publishers, 2009, 2010, 2011).

26 Elisabeth Kubler-Ross, M.D, *On Life after Death* (New York: Crown Publishing, 2008).

27 Ervin Laszlo and Anthony Peake, *The Immortal Mind* (Rochester: Inner Traditions, 2014).

28 Moriah Rhame-Brock, *How to Be a Happy Medium* (Chicago: Pendragon Publishing, Inc., 2004).

29 Anne Lamott, *Help, Thanks, Wow: The Three Essential Prayers* (New York: Riverhead Books, 2012).

30 Eckhart Tolle, *A New Earth: Awakening to Your Life's Purpose* (New York: Penguin, 2005).

ABOUT THE AUTHOR

 **P**enny Blue North is a songwriter, poet, author, playwright, and creator. She has composed more than a thousand songs and authored the novel *Fic-tio-nary*, the musical *Diva(s)!*, several children's books, and numerous nonfiction works. She also invented the board games *The Most* and *Don't Miss the Bus!* Penny earned a BSGS in English from Northwestern University and an MFA in creative writing from National University. Penny lives in Iowa with her creations, her daughter, "Dan/Phil," and "Merry Christmas." Find more at pennybluenorth.com

CPSIA information can be obtained
at www.ICGtesting.com
Printed in the USA
BVHW040524220223
658921BV00002BA/253